# POCKET **ROUGH GUIDE**
# PEMBROKESHIRE

written and researched by
**OWEN MORTON**

# CONTENTS

## A note to readers

At Rough Guides, we always strive to bring you the most up-to-date information. This book was produced during a period of continuing uncertainty caused by the Covid-19 pandemic, so please note that content is more subject to change than usual. We recommend checking the latest restrictions and official guidance.

# PEMBROKESHIRE

The fifth largest county in Wales, Pembrokeshire offers huge variety, from rugged beaches to the genteel and welcoming towns of Tenby and St Davids via medieval fortresses. It's ideal walking country, with the Pembrokeshire Coast Path offering stunning views at every turn, and there's a chance of spotting some of the county's extensive wildlife, such as seals, puffins and maybe even porpoises. With a huge number of excellent restaurants and cafés serving up tasty local food, it's not surprising that Pembrokeshire is considered one of the UK's top holiday destinations.

Tenby's North Beach

Pembrokeshire has a long history that's left considerable evidence behind: you can't fail to spot its traces on even the shortest visit to the county. The Neolithic burial chambers and hill forts that dot the landscape bear witness to the area's earliest inhabitants, and the early Christian period is memorialised by St Davids Cathedral. The medieval years were characterised by struggles between Norman invaders and the native Welsh, resulting in the construction of increasingly elaborate castles – in one of which, Pembroke, the man destined to become Henry VII, the founder of the Tudor dynasty, was born in 1457.

After seeing off the last invasion of Britain in 1797 – during which a French force landed at Fishguard – the county's focus shifted to industry, with coal mining becoming a particularly important activity. During the twentieth century, the dockyard at Pembroke Dock became a target for the Luftwaffe in the Second World War, and industrial development continued with the opening of oil refineries at Milford Haven and Rhoscrowther. Alongside this industrial activity, however, tourism in Pembrokeshire began to develop in the early nineteenth century, led

Coasteering near St Davids

by Sir William Paxton's drive to develop Tenby as a seaside resort. By the early twenty-first century, Pembrokeshire was attracting an estimated 7 million visitors per year. It's easy to see why Pembrokeshire is such a popular destination: it's a delightful corner of the country with a huge variety of attractions for tourists. Perhaps the most obvious is the abundance of fantastic beaches: all around the county, you'll find

## When to visit

Pembrokeshire has a mild climate year-round, tending to experience warm sunny weather throughout the summer months, generally from June to September, which is the period that sees the most visitors, particularly in the UK's school holidays. Outside these months you'll find the county quieter, with generally reliable weather during May and October, though it's not uncommon to enjoy warm days even in March and April. The winter tends to be mild: rain is fairly common, but snowfall is unlikely. If you're hoping to relax on the beach or visit the county's family-focused attractions, then the summer is the best time to come as many places close during the winter. However, if you're here for walking or water activities, there's a decent argument for visiting out of season, when accommodation prices are lower and the ocean throws up larger waves for surfing or bodyboarding. Bring a wetsuit, though! If you want to avoid crowds but still enjoy a strong chance of fine weather, the shoulder season of April and May is a good choice.

superb expanses of golden sands, lapped by clear water and backed by stunning scenery. In many cases – such as Whitesands Bay and Freshwater West – their western-facing aspects make them ideal for watersports, with the waves coming in off the Atlantic resulting in perfect conditions for surfing and bodyboarding. Other beaches, like Broad Haven and Barafundle Bay, are much more sheltered and their waters are safer, making them ideal for families with young children. Beaches aside, Pembrokeshire offers plenty of other reasons to get outdoors, primary among them the Pembrokeshire Coast Path which runs the entire length of the county's coastline from Amroth to Poppit Sands, only veering inland to avoid the firing range at Castlemartin. Walking the full path will take about two weeks and is a rewarding expedition, but it's also easy to pick and choose particularly attractive sections: above all, don't miss the route around the Marloes headland or the more rugged trail at Strumble Head.

If the weather doesn't favour you, there's plenty to do other than walking beaches and coast paths:

history lovers will enjoy exploring the county's castles – Pembroke and Carew are particular highlights – and will also get a lot out of visits to great museums such as the town museum at Narberth. For families, there are several excellent attractions that will keep children happy on non-beach days, including the Dinosaur Park, Folly Farm and, of course, Oakwood, the largest theme park in Wales.

After packing so much into your days, you're going to need something good to eat, and fortunately, Pembrokeshire excels in this area too. Naturally, given its extensive coastline, fish and seafood are plentiful and high quality – make sure to try some local crab or lobster – and there are abundant excellent fish and chip shops too. Pubs throughout the county offer great local food, and if you fancy splashing out, there are numerous top-notch restaurants to choose from, particularly around Narberth. There's such a wealth of things to do in Pembrokeshire that you could easily fill a two-week holiday and barely scratch the surface. For a fantastic trip with a great variety of attractions, it's hard to think of a better destination.

Lobster roll at Café Môr

# Where to...

## Shop

Most shops in Pembrokeshire are independent, though if you're looking for high-street chain outlets you'll be able to find a few (small) options in Haverfordwest and Tenby. Many of the county's towns specialise in boutique shops selling great homeware, clothing and gifts: Narberth is particularly blessed with such places, though Newport and St Davids give it a run for its money. St Davids is also the best place in the county to shop for surf gear, with good options to be found in Saundersfoot and Tenby too. Places selling local food and drink are common: there are great delis in St Davids, Fishguard, Narberth and Newport, and it's not hard to find shops stocking Welsh whisky, gin and wine. There's also a thriving local art scene, so in most villages of any size there'll be a place selling watercolours of Pembrokeshire views.

**OUR FAVOURITES: Unsunghero, see page 29. Golden Sheaf Gallery, see page 60. The Gourmet Pig, see page 66. The Gallery Yr Oriel, see page 74.**

## Eat

There are many upmarket restaurants to be found across Pembrokeshire, and a huge number of pubs to choose from too, serving up tasty locally sourced food. The most obvious is, of course, the fish and seafood caught in the waters around the county. Fish and chips – whether from a restaurant, a pub or a chippy – is invariably a great choice, and there are plenty of places to find crab or lobster. Meat eaters are also well catered for, with Welsh lamb featuring heavily on menus across the county, and there are often great beef options too. Vegetarians may fare a little less well, with many places offering only one or two unimaginative choices, though towns such as Narberth and Milford Haven do have more on offer. If you're looking for international options, there's not a huge choice, but you'll find Italian places in most of the main towns, as well as a fair number of Indian restaurants and the occasional Chinese.

**OUR FAVOURITES: The Shed Bistro, see page 30. Café Môr, see page 46. Ferry Inn, see page 75.**

## Drink

It's not hard to find a great pub in Pembrokeshire: all across the county, there are lovely welcoming pubs, often in small villages, where you'll be able to settle in for a drink. You're less likely to come across trendy wine bars, though a couple of places in Tenby and Newport are decent choices, and you could also consider visiting the Cwm Deri vineyard (see page ). Coffee shops and cafés are very common, many of them to be found in scenic spots where you can enjoy an excellent brew while gazing out across fantastic views.

**OUR FAVOURITES: The Sloop Inn, see page 31. Runwayskiln, see page 39. The Stackpole Inn, see page 47. The Carew Inn, see page 55.**

# Pembrokeshire at a glance

*ST GEORGE'S CHANNEL*

## Fishguard and around p.62.
Take a walk around Fishguard's attrac
harbour before exploring its interestin
history and enjoying the marvellous vie
from Strumble Head.

## St Davids and around p.24.
Visit Britain's smallest city, St Davids,
and take in its beautiful cathedral,
before exploring stretches of gorgeous
coastal paths or surfing on windswept
beaches.

## Haverfordwest and around p.32.
Beautiful beaches are easy to find
along the sweep of St Brides Bay and
around the Dale peninsula, and don't
miss the excellent boat trips around
the islands of Skomer and Skokholm.

## Pembroke and around p.40.
One of Wales' finest castles awaits
you in Pembroke, while the peninsula
to the town's south offers some of the
county's best beaches.

*Cardigan Bay*

*Fishguard Bay*

Sea Môr
Aquarium

Fishguard
Fort

Goodwick

Fishguard

Melin
Tregwynt

Dyffryn
Fernant
Garden

Abermawr
Beach

Scleddau

Mathry

Trecwn

Trefin

Letterston

Little
Newcastle

Porthgain

Abereiddy

Croes-goch

Newton

Wolf's Castle

Carnhedryn
Uchaf

Haycastle
Cross

*Whitesands
Bay*

St Davids

Dr Beynon's
Bug Farm

St Non's
Chapel

Solva

Brawdy

*Ramsey Island*

Newgale

Spitta

Roch

Scolto
Man

Camrose

Crundale

Nolton Haven

**Haverfordwest and around p.32.**

Sutton

Haverfordwest

Broad Haven

Little Haven

Johnston

Llangwm

*Skomer Island*

Dale Sailing
Boat Trips

Musselwick
Beach

Herbrandston

Milford Haven
Museum

Martin's Haven

Milford
Haven

Cledda
Bridge

Albion Sands

Dale

Neyland

Marloes
Sands

Pembroke

*Skokholm Island*

St Ann's
Head

*West
Angle
Bay*

Chapel Bay Fort
& Museum

Angle

*Angle
Bay*

Pembroke
Dock

Pembroke
Heritage C

Rhoscrowther

Pembrok

**Pembroke and around p.40.**

Freshwater
West Beach

Newton

Warren

Stackpo

Stackpole Estate
Bosherston Lily Ponds

Sta

Bosherston

St Govan's Chapel
(for access to
Castlemartin Range)

Poppit Sands
Cardigan
St Dogmaels Abbey ♦
Welsh Wildlife Centre ♦
St Dogmaels
Moylgrove
Cilgerran Castle
Cilgerran
Trewilym
Abercych
Nevern Castle ♙♦
Church of St Brynach ♙♦†
Rhoshill
Nevern
Castell Henllys Iron Age Village
Boncath
Pentre Ifan
Blaenffos
Bwlch-y-groes
Cilgwyn
Tŷ Canol Woods
Crosswell
West Cilrhedyn
Penlan Uchaf Gardens
Crymych
Tafarn-y-bwlch
Tegryn
Mynachlog-ddu
Hermon
Greenway
Rosebush
Glandwr
Maenclochog
Pembrokeshire Llamas
Llandissilio
Bletherston

**Newport and around** p.68.
Explore the stark beauty of the Preseli Hills and a more remote stretch of the coastal path, before checking out the region's fascinating Iron Age heritage.

Llawhaden Castle ♙♦
Llanddewi Velfrey
Llawhaden
Narberth
Clerkenhill Adventure Farm
Princes Gate
Oakwood Theme Park ♦
Wild Lakes ♦
Castle Gardens
Colby Woodland Garden
Cwm Deri Vineyard
Folly Farm Adventure Park and Zoo ♦
Cresswell
Kilgetty Ironworks
Amroth
Carew Mill
Carew Castle ♙♦
Heatherton World of Activities
Saundersfoot
Carew
Dinosaur Park ♦
Manor Wildlife Park
Tenby
Manorbier Castle ♙♦
Manorbier
Manorbier Beach
Church Door Cove
Caldey Island

**Narberth and around** p.56.
Fine dining and boutique shopping is the name of the game in Narberth, but you'll also have the chance to take in some fine medieval castles and visit Wales' largest theme park.

**Tenby and around** p.48.
The lovely seaside resort of Tenby boasts great sandy beaches, and is in easy reach of fun kid-friendly destinations such as the Dinosaur Park and Manor Wildlife Park.

*BRISTOL CHANNEL*

# 15

# Things not to miss

It's not possible to see everything that Pembrokeshire has to offer in one trip – and we don't suggest you try. What follows is a selective taste of the county's highlights, from beautiful beaches and stunning coastal walks to magnificent medieval castles and family-friendly activities.

## > Pembroke Castle
See page 40
Castles don't come much better than Pembroke's: a perfectly preserved gatehouse with dark and atmospheric passageways to explore, a huge keep offering great views, and a creepy cave underground.

## < Marloes
See page 36
Pembrokeshire is blessed with many gorgeous beaches, but Marloes takes the crown; its golden sands and clear waters enjoy the dramatic backdrop of Gateholm Island.

## ∨ St Davids Cathedral
See page 24
Hidden in a valley to protect it from Viking raiders, St Davids Cathedral is a grand and historic building found in Britain's smallest city. Check out too the adjacent ruined palace.

## < **Skomer Island**
### See page 36

Keen wildlife spotters should take a boat trip to Skomer Island where, depending on the time of year, you may see hundreds of puffins and other sea birds, or huge numbers of seals and their pups.

## ∨ **Neolithic heritage**
### See page 72

The ancient inhabitants of Pembrokeshire left many traces behind: explore impressive hill forts and burial chambers at Castell Henllys and Pentre Ifan.

### ∧ Bosherston Lily Ponds
**See page 44**
The beautiful lily ponds at
Bosherston are a perfect place
for an easy afternoon stroll, with
the added bonus of a great beach
halfway along the route.

### ‹ Oakwood
**See page 57**
Ramp up the adrenaline with a
visit to Wales' largest theme park,
with a range of rides suitable for
thrill seekers of all ages.

## ∧ Strumble Head

**See page 63**

The coast path around Strumble Head offers awesome views all the way along the north coast of Pembrokeshire; for a truly unparalleled panorama, climb to the summit of Garn Fawr.

## ∨ Freshwater West

**See page 45**

If you want to get active on the water, there are few better beaches than Freshwater West, which is ideal for surfing, bodyboarding, kite-surfing and much more.

### ∧ Dinosaur Park
**See page 52**
For a fun day out with the kids, there are few better choices than this great dinosaur-themed park featuring plenty of activities and dinos hiding around every corner.

### ‹ Eating in Narberth
**See page 60**
From locally sourced gourmet meals to fantastic Spanish tapas, by way of alcoholic ice cream, the food on offer in Narberth is some of the best in Pembrokeshire.

< **St Brynach's Church**
See page 69
The dark and atmospheric churchyard of St Brynach's in Nevern is home to a collection of intriguing artefacts: an intricately carved Celtic cross, a fifth-century Rosetta Stone, and a bleeding yew tree.

⌄ **Welsh Wildlife Centre**
See page 72
Look out for a wide variety of birds and mammals (including otters) from the hides and boardwalks of the excellent Welsh Wildlife Centre.

THINGS NOT TO MISS

# Day one in Pembrokeshire

**Solva.** See page 27. Have a look around this attractive village, making sure to check out the quaint artist studios and taking a relaxing walk along the lovely cliff path past the harbour towards Newgale.

**St Davids**. See page 24. Spend the rest of the morning exploring Britain's smallest city, taking in its famously beautiful cathedral and the nearby Bishop's Palace with its gorgeous rose window. The attractive streets of St Davids are also worth a wander, offering great boutique shopping opportunities and delicious snacks.

🍴 **Lunch**. See page 29. Make a beeline for the excellent deli, St Davids Food & Wine, to browse the huge range of local produce nd pick some up supplies for a picnic. Take your goodies down to Whitesands Bay to enjoy on the beach.

**Whitesands Bay**. See page 26. Luxuriate in an afternoon on the beach, enjoying the feeling of the sand between your toes, building sandcastles and paddling. The more adventurous (and the less stuffed with picnic) can take the chance to get active in the water, swimming, surfing or bodyboarding.

**Abereiddy**. See page 28. Head along the northern coast to Abereiddy and take in the gorgeous turquoise-green waters of the Blue Lagoon – and jump in, if you feel brave enough!

🍴 **Dinner**. See page 30. Take the gorgeous cliff path from Abereiddy to Porthgain and treat yourself to an excellent supper of fish and chips at the Shed Bistro. Walk it off on the return trip to Abereiddy, enjoying panoramic views of evening sunlight on the sea.

Solva

Whitesands Bay

Seafood at The Shed

# Day two in Pembrokeshire

**Pembroke Castle**. See page 40. Kick off your day by exploring the towers and battlements of Pembroke Castle, one of the best castles in Wales, making sure to take in the fine view from the top of the keep.

**Freshwater West**. See page 45. Head over to Freshwater West, a brilliant beach backed by grassy sand dunes, and enjoy a morning swimming or kite-surfing in the sea.

**Lunch**. See page 46. You'll no doubt be feeling peckish after an active morning, so head up to Freshwater West's car park, where you'll find Café Môr, which offers some of the best beach food you'll find in Pembrokeshire. The lobster and crab rolls are excellent.

**Bosherston**. See page 44. Enjoy a relaxing walk at the charming Bosherston Lily Ponds, which in summer are carpeted with colourful flowers. Look out for the abundant wildlife here – you could catch a glimpse of herons, owls and even otters if you're eagle-eyed and lucky.

**Broad Haven South.** See page 44. The walk at Bosherston will lead you to the lovely Broad Haven South beach, a perfect spot for a quick dip in the clear (but bracingly chilly!) waters overlooked by the dramatic Church Rock.

**Tenby**. See page 48. Take a meandering evening promenade along Tenby's colourful seafront, perhaps stopping to admire the fine view from the summit of Castle Hill.

**Dinner**. See pages 54 and 55. Tenby has some great restaurants to choose from, including the excellent Blue Ball. Finish up with a nightcap at one of the town's friendly pubs, such as the Harbwr Brewery.

ITINERARIES

Pembroke Castle

Café Môr

Sunset over Tenby

# Pembrokeshire for families

Pembrokeshire is a perfect destination for a family holiday, offering a huge range of great activities that'll keep children entertained.

**Oakwood**. See page 57. Wales' biggest theme park will keep children and teenagers (and adults!) happy all day, with rides ranging from the uterly tame to the totally terrifying.

**Boat trips.** See page 35. The boat outings available from the Pembrokeshire Islands company at Martin's Haven range from gentle cruises around Skomer Island to fast and exciting rigid inflatable rides that aren't for the faint of heart.

**Folly Farm Adventure Park & Zoo.** See page 58. This combined petting farm, zoo and small theme park is perfect for younger children in particular, offering the chance to get up close and personal with a fine selection of animals. There's a great playground for running about in afterwards.

**Broad Haven.** See page 33. There are great beaches all over Pembrokeshire, but Broad Haven is probably the most family-friendly of them all, with a huge flat expanse of golden sand on which kids can safely run around and let off steam. The beach is lapped by calm waves, with shops and facilities just a short stroll away.

**Dinosaur Park.** See page 52. Take a walk through the woods at Dinosaur Park and come face to face with a whole gang of prehistoric beasties, then have a go on the park's rides or enjoy a round of dinosaur golf.

**Sea Môr Aquarium.** See page 63. Explore Pembrokeshire's marine wildlife at this great aquarium, where knowledgeable and friendly staff lead tours that offer great hands-on experiences for kids.

Oakwood rollercoaster

Ramsey Isand Boat Trip

Penguins at Folly Farm

# Budget Pembrokeshire

It's easy to enjoy Pembrokeshire without breaking the bank, as many of its myriad attractions are free or very cheap to experience.

**Beaches**. There's no charge for visiting any of Pembrokeshire's excellent beaches, though you will sometimes need to pay a minimal parking fee. Particular highlights include Marloes Sands (see page 36) and Freshwater West (see page 45), but it's difficult to go wrong whichever beach you choose.

**Historic Pembrokeshire**. Although some of the top-hitting castles charge for entry, there are plenty of historic sites across the county that are free to visit. Stop by the ruins of Llawhaden Castle (see page 58), seek out the many Neolithic burial chambers and hill forts scattered across the Preseli Hills (see page 72), and make a visit to Fishguard to check out the fabulous Last Invasion tapestry (see page 62).

**The Coast Path**. Stretching right round from Amroth (see page 51) to Poppit Sands (see page 71), the Pembrokeshire Coast Path is an unbroken walking trail that hugs the shoreline of the entire county – and it's entirely free to walk. Tackle the whole thing over two weeks, or choose particularly attractive sections to enjoy: try the Abereiddy to Porthgain route (see page 28), or the rugged stretch around Ceibwr Bay (see page 71).

**Wildlife spotting**. Pembrokeshire offers some excellent wildlife spotting opportunities, and there are plenty of places you can see the local fauna for free. Try the Deer Park at St Martin's Haven (see page 35), from which you'll be able to spot seals with their pups in August and September, head to the Welsh Wildlife Centre (see page 72) for great bird-watching, or visit Bosherston Lily Ponds (see page 44) for a chance of seeing otters.

Marloes Sands

Llawhaden Castle

On the Coast Path

# PLACES

Bishop's Palace, St Davids

# St Davids and around

The UK's smallest city by a considerable distance, St Davids is in many ways the cultural heart of Pembrokeshire. Its focal point is the impressive cathedral, which is the spiritual and ecclesiastical centre of Wales: you'll find here the shrine of St David, Wales' patron saint, which has attracted pilgrims for nearly 1500 years. The city is an arty place with a couple of big touristic hitters – the cathedral, of course, and the nearby Bishop's Palace – but you should also make time to explore the surrounding countryside and coastline: there are several magnificent beaches in this area, and the stretches of the Pembrokeshire Coastal Path on both the north and south sides of the St Davids headland are beautiful.

## St Davids Cathedral

MAP P.26
The Close, St Davids, SA62 6RD. 01437
720202, www.stdavidscathedral.org.uk.
Mon–Sat 8.30am–5pm, Sun 12.45–5pm. £3

donation requested; guided tours £4.
Nestled at the bottom of the hill from the centre, St Davids cathedral is approached via a set of 39 steps from the fourteenth-century Tower

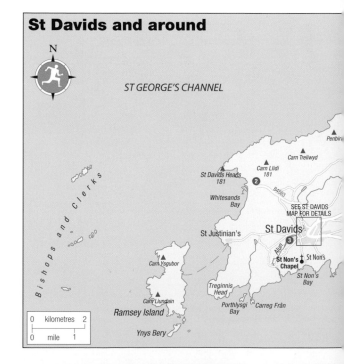

**St Davids and around**

N

ST GEORGE'S CHANNEL

Penbir

Carn Treliwyd

Carn Llidi
181

St Davids Heads
181

2

B4583

Whitesands
Bay

SEE ST DAVIDS
MAP FOR DETAILS

St Justinian's

St Davids

3

Afon

St Non's
Chapel

St Non's

Carn Ysgubor

St Non's
Bay

Treginnis
Head

Carn Llundain

Porthlysgi
Bay

Carreg Frân

Ramsey Island

Ynys Bery

0    kilometres    2

0    mile    1

Gate. It's an attractive building from the outside, but its true treasures are to be found inside: in particular, check out the exquisite medieval misericords under the choir seats, which include depictions of dragons and other legendary beasts, as well as a boatload of seasick pilgrims. Make sure not to miss the presbytery – where you'll find the tomb of King Henry VII's father, Edmund Tudor – and take a moment to admire the intricate latticed oak roof of the cathedral's nave.

## Bishop's Palace

MAP P.26

The Close, St Davids, SA62 6PE. 01437 720517, www.cadw.gov.wales/visit/places-to-visit/st-davids-bishops-palace. Daily Mar–Jun & Sep–Oct 9.30am–5pm; Jul–Aug 9.30am–6pm; Nov–Feb 10am–4pm. £4.50.

Just across from the cathedral, you'll find the extensive remains of the medieval Bishop's Palace, which was largely built under

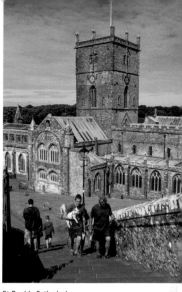

St Davids Cathedral

the direction of the Bishops Beck (1280–93) and Gower (1328–47). Don't miss the impressive great

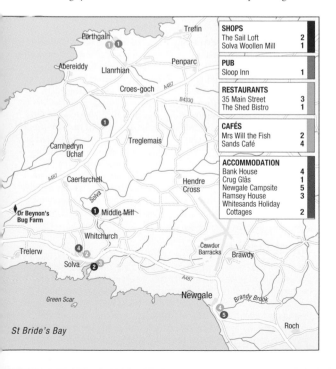

| SHOPS | |
|---|---|
| The Sail Loft | 2 |
| Solva Woollen Mill | 1 |

| PUB | |
|---|---|
| Sloop Inn | 1 |

| RESTAURANTS | |
|---|---|
| 35 Main Street | 3 |
| The Shed Bistro | 1 |

| CAFÉS | |
|---|---|
| Mrs Will the Fish | 2 |
| Sands Café | 4 |

| ACCOMMODATION | |
|---|---|
| Bank House | 4 |
| Crug Glâs | 1 |
| Newgale Campsite | 5 |
| Ramsey House | 3 |
| Whitesands Holiday Cottages | 2 |

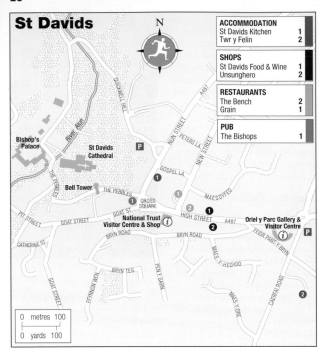

**St Davids**

N

| ACCOMMODATION | |
|---|---|
| St Davids Kitchen | 1 |
| Twr y Felin | 2 |

| SHOPS | |
|---|---|
| St Davids Food & Wine | 1 |
| Unsunghero | 2 |

| RESTAURANTS | |
|---|---|
| The Bench | 2 |
| Grain | 1 |

| PUB | |
|---|---|
| The Bishops | 1 |

Bishop's Palace

St Davids Cathedral

Bell Tower

River Alun

THE PEBBLES

PIT STREET

GOAT STREET

CATHERINE ST

GOAT STREET

DWRKWELL HILL

CROSS SQUARE

GOAT ST

BRYN ROAD

BRYN ROAD

GOSPEL LA

HIGH STREET

A487

NUN STREET

PETERS LA

NEW STREET

A487

MAESDYFED

National Trust Visitor Centre & Shop

Oriel y Parc Gallery & Visitor Centre

MAES Y HEDYDD

EFFINNON WEN

BRYN TEG

PEN Y GARN

MAES Y FFORE

FEIDR PANTY-Y-BRYN

CAEBAI ROAD

0 metres 100
0 yards 100

hall, with its gorgeous rose window. There are plenty of information boards around the site which give context to the ruins, including audio recordings and games that make the history of the palace pleasingly accessible for children – have you ever wondered what job you'd have been best suited to in medieval times?

## Whitesands Bay

MAP P.24

The gorgeous Whitesands Bay lives up to its name – it's a perfect expanse of bleached white sand that's a popular and easily accessible spot for a great day out at the beach. The waves here are perfect for surfers and bodyboarders, and there are plenty of facilities available, including a café, toilets and a decent-sized car park. To the north of the beach, the rugged St Davids Head offers short walks with fantastic views from the summit, and the Pembrokeshire Coastal Path here takes you past a Neolithic burial chamber known as Arthur's Quoit.

## Saint David

The city of St Davids is, of course, named after Saint David, the patron saint of Wales. David is thought to have lived in the sixth century, and spent his life preaching and founding monastic houses across Wales, England and Brittany. He is credited with having performed a number of miracles, including raising a hill on which the village of Llanddewi Brefi in Ceredigion now stands. His tomb can be seen in the presbytery of St Davids Cathedral.

## Ramsey Island

MAP P.24

Departing from Whitesands Bay or St Justinian's, boat trips to the RSPB-administered Ramsey Island are a must for those interested in Pembrokeshire's wildlife. The island is home to many different species of sea bird – visit in late spring to see puffins – as well as hosting seals and their pups in autumn. You can land on the island with boat trips run by Thousand Island Expeditions (Cross Square, St Davids, SA62 6SL, 01437 721721, www. thousandislands.co.uk, £22–60), though there are plenty of operators who offer trips around the island on boats or rigid inflatable craft.

## St Non's Chapel

MAP P.24

According to early Christian tradition, St Non gave birth to St David at this spot amid a tumultuous storm, after which a spring opened at her feet and a calm light descended around her. The site became a popular pilgrimage destination, and the remains of the thirteenth-century chapel can still be seen here. It's on an attractive section of the Pembrokeshire Coastal Path, just a short walk to the pleasant Caerfai Beach to the east or to the turquoise waters of Porth Clais Harbour to the west.

## Dr Beynon's Bug Farm

MAP P.24

Lower Harglodd Farm, St Davids, SA62 6BX. 07966 956357, www.thebugfarm. co.uk. Apr–Oct Thu–Sun, Nov–Mar Sat–Sun, 10.30am–4.30pm. £6.50.

Just outside St Davids, Dr Beynon's Bug Farm is a great afternoon out, involving a bug zoo housing a wide variety of mini-beasts, as well as a fascinating museum giving an insight into the little critters, a walled garden and trails to follow across the estate. There's also a restaurant, serving sustainably produced fare which usually includes edible insects, though at time of writing changes in food regulations resulting from Brexit meant that bugs were temporarily off the menu – keep an eye on the website for updates.

## Solva

MAP P.24

Pretty little Solva, a picture-postcard village about three miles east of St Davids, is worth a stop to browse its attractive shops – there are plenty of opportunities to pick up a souvenir here. Just outside the village on the Pembrokeshire Coastal Path heading east, you'll come across the remains of several lime kilns, a reminder of the village's industrial heritage. Continue the walk to Newgale to enjoy one of the loveliest stretches of the Coastal Path.

## Newgale

MAP P.24

Newgale offers a vast and easily accessible sandy beach that's popular with swimmers, paddleboarders, bodyboarders and surfers; there are facilities including toilets, cafés and a car park, as well as a shop from which you can hire water sports equipment, at the northern end of the beach.

Whitesands Bay

## Asser and King Alfred the Great

As a centre of Christianity and learning, the early medieval St Davids produced several noteworthy scholars. Perhaps the most famous was a monk named Asser, who was considered so learned that he was recruited by King Alfred the Great of Wessex to join his court. While there, Asser wrote a biography of Alfred, which remains one of the main sources of information on Alfred's reign and personality.

## Abereiddy

MAP P.24

Northeast along the coast from St Davids, the cove of Abereiddy was once the site of a slate quarry, which closed in 1910 and was later dynamited for safety reasons. The resultant hole has filled with sea water which is tinted turquoise thanks to the minerals in the surrounding rocks and is now referred to as the Blue Lagoon. It's a great spot for fossil hunters, and for those of an adventurous bent, coasteering companies in the vicinity – including Celtic Quest (01348 837337, www. celticquestcoasteering.com) – offer the opportunity to leap from the cliffs into the lagoon's deep (and cold) water.

## Porthgain

MAP P.24

The walk along the Pembrokeshire Coastal Path from Abereiddy to Porthgain is one of the most interesting in the county, offering fantastic views across bays and beaches as well as taking you past the remains of the area's industrial past in the form of abandoned quarry buildings. It's even possible to trace the line of a former narrow-gauge railway on the cliffs.

Porthgain itself is a small but lovely village with a pretty harbour. The western side is dominated by the remains of a former quarrying building, but you'll perhaps be more interested in the Shed: a former engine repairs shop is now a venue for excellent fish and chips.

The harbour at Porthgain

The Sail Loft in Solva

# Shops

### The Sail Loft, Solva

MAP P.24

19 Main Street, Solva, SA62 6UU. 01437
721114, www.solvasailloft.com. Mon–Sat
10.30am–5.30pm, Sun 11am–5pm.
A small art gallery showcasing
pretty watercolour paintings
by local artist Simon Swinfield,
among others, the Sail Loft has a
lovely variety of souvenirs and gifts
ranging from pottery to glassware,
as well as prints of the gallery's
artworks.

### Solva Woollen Mill

MAP P.24

Middle Mill, Solva, SA62 6XD. 01437
721112, www.solvawoollenmill.co.uk.
Jul–Sep Mon–Sat 9.30am–5.30pm,
Sun 2pm–5.30pm, Oct–Jun Mon–Fri
9.30am–5.30pm.
Even if you're not in the market
for the lovely woollen rugs and
throws that are produced here, it's
worth visiting this long-established
woollen mill to see the still-working
waterwheel (an attraction in itself!)
and treat yourself to a coffee and
cake at the tearoom.

### St Davids Food & Wine

MAP P.26

High Street, St Davids, SA62 6SB. 01437
721948, www.stdavidsdeli.co.uk. Mon–Sat
10am–3pm.
Perfect for picking up an edible
souvenir, or simply stocking up for
a picnic lunch, this little deli has a
huge range of tasty local produce.
There's a particularly fine selection
of cheeses, and it could take a while
to work through the thirty or so
Welsh beers on sale.

### Unsunghero, St Davids

MAP P.26

28B High Street, St Davids, SA62 6SD.
01437 729437, https://unsungherosurf.
co.uk. Daily 9am–5pm.
There are several places in St Davids
to buy surfing essentials, from
boards to wetsuits, but Unsunghero
is the pick of the bunch, thanks
to the hugely knowledgeable staff.
They also offer great coffee, widely
considered the best in St Davids.

# Restaurants

### 35 Main Street

MAP P.24

35 Main St, Solva, SA62 6UT. 01437 729236, www.35mainstreet.co.uk. Daily Apr–Oct 10am–9pm, Nov–Mar Sun–Mon & Thu 10am–5pm & Fri–Sat 10am–9pm.
Café by day and restaurant by night, 35 Main Street serves up great food whatever time of day you swing by. The breakfast menu (served until 11.30am) makes it especially worth a visit, and the lunch and evening menus offer a wide range of meals of which the fish-based choices are particularly good.

### Grain
MAP P.26
1 High Street, St. Davids SA62 6SA. 01437 454321, www.grain.wales. Tue–Sun 10am–3pm & 5pm–10pm.
This rustic wooden chalet-style place serves up fantastic wood-fired pizza with innovative toppings – make sure to try the Welsh-themed 'Land of our Fathers' with leek and local Perl Las blue cheese – alongside excellent craft beers. It's deservedly popular, so it may be worth booking ahead.

### The Shed Bistro
MAP P.24

56 Llanrhian Road, Porthgain, SA62 5BN. 01348 831518, www.theshedporthgain.co.uk. Daily noon–3pm & 5–8.45pm.
Housed in the former machine workshop on Porthgain's harbour, the Shed Bistro offers a great menu of local fish and seafood. It's particularly renowned for its fish and chips and is justly popular – be prepared to queue on warm summer evenings. Takeaway is sometimes available, but not always – so if this is your plan, it could be worth checking in advance.

## Cafés

### The Bench
MAP P.26
Corner High Street and New Street, St Davids, SA62 6SB. 07855 327196, www.facebook.com/pg/benchcafe. Daily Apr–Oct 9.30am–6pm.
On a hot day, there really is nothing better than cooling down with a cone of the best gelato in Pembrokeshire. The ice cream at The Bench is made with local organic milk and comes in an amazing range of flavours such

Surf shop in St Davids

Fish and chips at The Shed

as Kinder Bueno or gin and elderflower.

## Mrs Will the Fish

MAP P.24

Parc Benny, Panteg Road, Solva, SA62 6TN. 01437 721571, www.facebook.com/MrsWillTheFish. Mon–Wed & Fri–Sat 9am–5pm.

It might not look fancy, and it might have a rather odd name, but don't be tempted to overlook this place; if you're looking for superbly dressed crab, lobster and other local seafood, you're unlikely to find finer anywhere in Pembrokeshire. Takeaway only.

## Sands Café

MAP P.24

Main road, Newgale, SA62 6AS. 01437 729222, www.facebook.com/sandsnewgale. Daily 9.30am–4.30pm.

A great place just off the beach at Newgale, serving up baguettes, panini, espresso, ice creams and smoothies, plus light meals such as green pea and pesto soup or smoked mackerel pâté. Bring a reuseable cup for a reduction on the price of a warming takeaway coffee.

# Pubs

## The Bishops

MAP P.26

22-23 Cross Sq, St Davids, SA62 6SL. 01437 720422, www.thebish.co.uk. Daily 11.30am–midnight.

Right in the middle of St Davids, the lovely Bishops is a perfect place to stop for a drink or a pub meal. The menu includes all the pub classics, with the fish and chips coming particularly recommended. Sit in the pub's cosy interior on a cold evening, or if it's warmer you can enjoy views of the cathedral from the outdoor seating area.

## Sloop Inn

MAP P.24

Porthgain, SA62 5BN. 01348 831449, www.sloop.co.uk. Tue–Sat 9.30am–11pm, Sun 9.30am–5pm.

This lovely eighteenth-century pub has a perfect terrace on which to while away the evening, or if it's a cooler day the interior is beautifully rustic. The food is good – local fish and seafood usually take top billing on the specials menu, and they also do a very fine Sunday roast.

# Haverfordwest and around

Pembrokeshire's county town, Haverfordwest (Hwlffordd), is hardly the most attractive of places, but you'll no doubt find yourself passing though here, and if you've got time to spare it's worth a quick explore to try to get a sense of its long history. Its ancient origins are obscure, though there may have been a Roman presence here, and it was certainly an important place in the medieval and Tudor periods, though it then fell into decline in the seventeenth century thanks to the Civil War and an outbreak of plague. Haverfordwest could make a decent place to base yourself, but you're more likely to want to move on to the peninsula stretching southwest from here, which is arguably the most beautiful part of Pembrokeshire, with perfect beaches, gorgeous coast paths and fantastic wildlife-spotting opportunities.

## Haverfordwest Town Museum

MAP P.34
Castle St, Haverfordwest, SA61 2EF. 01437 763087, www.haverfordwest-town-museum. org.uk. Apr–Oct Mon–Sat 10am–4pm. £2.
In the imposing governor's house (1779) next to the castle is the

Boat trip to Skomer Island

Haverfordwest Town Museum, a motley collection of fairly interesting local history exhibits, such as the first ballot paper used here, Nelson's freedom of the borough charter, and lots of historical photos.

## Haverfordwest Castle

MAP P.34
Castle St, Haverfordwest, SA61 2EF. 01437 763087, www.haverfordwest-town-museum.org.uk. 24h. Free.
Haverfordwest's castle, initially built in the early twelfth century, looks impressive from the outside but is unlikely to detain you long if you venture inside: there's little left but the bare shell of the thirteenth-century inner ward.

## Haverfordwest Priory

MAP P.34
Quay St, Haverfordwest, SA61 1RZ. www.cadw.gov.wales/visit/places-to-visit/haverfordwest-priory. Daily 10am–4pm (officially, though can be accessed 24h). Free.
A quick amble around the ruins of Haverfordwest's Augustinian Priory, established around the year 1200 on the banks of the

Cleddau, makes for a reasonably interesting historical diversion if you find yourself with time to kill while in town. It is rather difficult to imagine the peaceful life of its inhabitants, though, given the proximity of the A4076 flyover.

## Welsh Spitfire Museum

MAP P.34

16 Bridge St, Haverfordwest, SA61 2AD. 01437 762512, www.welshspitfire.org. Mon–Sat 9.30am–4.30pm. Free.

Run by and largely for enthusiasts, the Welsh Spitfire Museum is home to the fuselage of a Spitfire VIII and numerous other parts of the plane, as well as a small collection of other World War II artefacts. The ultimate aim is to reassemble the plane and take it for a flight, and while that intention seems some way off realisation – as yet, the plane has no wings – it's worth a quick look around the collection in the meantime. The museum will be moving at an unspecified time in the future, as the building has been purchased by the council and is scheduled for demolition.

## Scolton Manor

MAP P.34

Near Bethlehem, SA62 5QL. 01437 731328, www.culture4pembrokeshire.co.uk/ content.asp?nav=8. Grounds Apr–Oct 9am–6pm, Nov–Mar 9am–4.30pm; Manor House Mon–Wed 11.30am–4.30pm. Free entry to grounds, parking charges apply (£3.50 for two hours); Manor House £3.50.

Scolton Manor Country Park makes for a diverting couple of hours' stop, particularly if you have kids with you who will enjoy the Welsh Myths and Legends Trail and the steam locomotive on display by the car park. There's also a pleasant walled garden here, as well as the Pembrokeshire Beekeeping Centre, which houses a small but interesting beekeeping exhibition and several beehives. The Manor house itself, built in 1842, is a stolid white-grey building; inside, it's been restored to show off the fine Victorian furnishings and décor upstairs and the rather more austere servants' quarters below.

## Broad Haven

MAP P.34

Five miles or so from Haverfordwest is the small but brash village of Broad Haven, blessed with a large sandy beach that's extremely easy to access. As such, it's a very popular holiday destination, with a slew of self-catering apartments to choose from. Sunsets over Broad Haven Beach, which faces directly west, are sublime. For those who hanker after active pursuits, the Pembrokeshire Coast Path heading north to Nolton Haven is an attractive leg stretcher; keep an eye out for the hobbit-hole-like house Malator, near Druidston, which is built into the cliffside and is visible from the path.

## Little Haven

MAP P.34

At low tide, you can walk south from Broad Haven Beach round the cliffs to the smaller beach at Little Haven, a charming village

Wales Coast Path near Broad Haven

# Between a Rock and a Hard Place: Pembrokeshire's Geology

Walking the Pembrokeshire Coastal Path, you'll quickly notice the many different types of rock on show in the cliffs and on the beaches here: red and grey sandstone and mudstone, grey limestone, black basalt, and occasionally layers of black coal, testifying to the industrial heritage of the area. In many spots, it's easy to see the different layers that have been exposed; sometimes these are flat and straight, such as the Three Chimneys on Marloes beach, while in other places – such as Little Haven beach or at Ceibwr Bay – the layers of rock are distorted and bent, evidence of the immense geological forces at work to create this landscape.

that makes a perfect base for exploring the area. The beach here is flat and sandy, with impressive geology on show in the rocks of the cliffs. Head along to the Point (up the path from the Swan Hotel) for lovely views of the beach and rugged coastline, or for a longer walk there's an easy and attractive

section of the Pembrokeshire Coast Path beginning here.

Note that if you're driving between Broad and Little Haven, the most direct road involves the hairpinniest of hairpin bends, which is aggravated by its 20% gradient; if you're not a confident driver, go the slightly longer way round via Walton West.

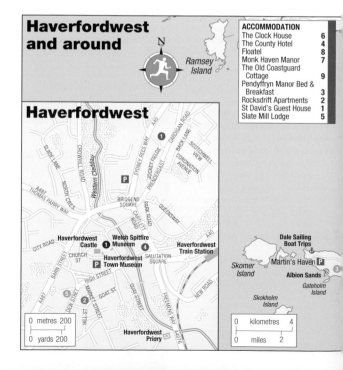

## Martin's Haven

MAP P.34

Martin's Haven offers only a small and stony beach, but it's worth visiting for two reasons: firstly, it's the departure point for boat trips (see page 36), and secondly, it offers access to a lovely short coastal walk around the Deer Park, a headland which is blessed with magnificent views out to Skomer and Skokholm Islands. Visit at the right time of year (between August and September) and you're likely to see seals and their pups on the rocky inaccessible beaches below you at the base of the headland. You should also take a good look at the channel running north to south between the headland and Skomer Island: this marks the boundary between the Irish Sea and the Bristol Channel, and it's sometimes possible to spot a dramatic change in sea level between the two.

As you take the road to or from Martin's Haven, it's worth a stop

Broad Haven surfing

at Musselwick Beach, a beautiful sandy expanse that's only accessible at low tide.

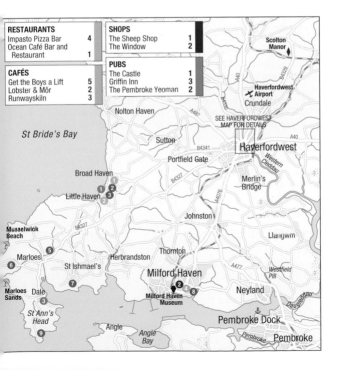

| RESTAURANTS | |
|---|---|
| Impasto Pizza Bar | 4 |
| Ocean Café Bar and Restaurant | 1 |

| CAFÉS | |
|---|---|
| Get the Boys a Lift | 5 |
| Lobster & Môr | 2 |
| Runwayskiln | 3 |

| SHOPS | |
|---|---|
| The Sheep Shop | 1 |
| The Window | 2 |

| PUBS | |
|---|---|
| The Castle | 1 |
| Griffin Inn | 3 |
| The Pembroke Yeoman | 2 |

Gateway to Marloes Sands

## Dale Sailing Boat Trips

MAP P.34

Martin's Haven, SA62 3BJ. 01646 603123,
www.pembrokeshire-islands.co.uk.
Roughly hourly departures. £15–45.

Martin's Haven is also the departure point for some of the best boat trips in Pembrokeshire. The nearby islands of Skomer, Skokholm and Grassholm are all excellent for birdwatching, and make great destinations for outings in boats, whether you choose a sedate trip around the islands or a high-octane rigid inflatable ride. It's possible to land on Skomer Island for the day, where – if you visit between May and July – you'll have the opportunity to see staggering numbers of puffins: it's an utterly delightful day trip and the puffins seem quite fearless as they happily meander across your path. Note that there are only very basic facilities on the island so you'll need to bring your own picnic. Booking in advance is essential.

## Marloes

MAP P.34

A strong contender for the most beautiful beach in Pembrokeshire, Marloes Sands is a ridiculously perfect place. Its mile-long stretch of golden sand is punctuated by picturesque jagged rocks, and the sea here is ideal for swimming and bodyboarding (best at low tide, so check the tide tables). It's also a great spot to study the region's fascinating

## Henry VII

As you walk the Pembrokeshire Coastal Path from Dale to St Ann's Head Lighthouse, you'll pass Mill Bay, where you may spot a plaque marking the place where Henry Tudor, Earl of Pembroke, landed in 1485 on his way to challenge Richard III for the throne of England. Henry's claim to the throne was rather tenuous, but he enjoyed a fair degree of support among the nobles, and his subsequent victory at Bosworth Field effectively ended the long-running strife of the Wars of the Roses.

geology: the Three Chimneys, about two-thirds of the way along the beach, testify to the massive mountain-building upheavals hundreds of millions of years ago.

Access to Marloes Sands is via a half mile pushchair-friendly path down from the National Trust operated car park, which can fill up in summer. If it's high tide, once you're there, you'll then need to turn left and head along the coast path for a further short distance to access the beach.

## Gateholm Island and Albion Sands

MAP P.34

The far right of Marloes Sands is dominated by the mass of Gateholm Island, where Iron Age hut circles, pottery and jewellery have been found and which seems to have been an ancient monastic community. When it's not high tide, it's possible – but not easy – to scramble up onto the summit.

Just past Gateholm Island, and only accessible at low tide, is Albion Sands, a small but gorgeous expanse of sandy beach which is perfect if you're seeking an isolated spot. It's named after the Albion, a paddle steamer which ran aground here in the nineteenth century – it's still possible to see parts of the unlucky ship poking above the water at low tide. Make sure to watch the clock while you're here – it's possible to get cut off by the tide.

## Dale and St Ann's Head

MAP P.34

The small village of Dale sits in a sheltered bay that looks straight across to Milford Haven, so oil refinery enthusiasts will enjoy the view from here. Others will perhaps be more tempted to visit Dale for its excellent watersports opportunities and boat trips: due to its sheltered location, Dale's bay makes the ideal place for spot of paddleboarding or kayaking. St Ann's Head, the promontory that stretches south from Dale, is a lovely and historically significant section of the Pembrokeshire Coastal Path.

## Milford Haven

MAP P.34

The town of Milford Haven – founded in 1790 by Quakers from Nantucket, brought here to work as whalers – is today notable largely for its enormous offshore oil refineries, which are hardly attractive but nevertheless oddly mesmerising. The town's waterfront, however, is a fairly lively spot, boasting a decent range of cafés and restaurants, and it's worth taking a quick wander through the small but pleasant public gardens that overlook the harbour.

## Milford Haven Museum

MAP P.34

The Marina, SA73 3AF. 01646 694496, www.facebook.com/MilfordHavenMuseum. Easter–Oct Mon–Sat 10.30am–4pm. £4.

The museum, which occupies the late-eighteenth-century Customs House, is worth a look for an overview of the town's history. It's most interesting for its exhibition on the role Milford Haven played during the World Wars, when massive convoys formed here.

Puffins on Skomer Island

# Shops

### The Sheep Shop

MAP P.34

32 Bridge Street, Haverfordwest, SA61 2AD. 01437 766844, www.sheepshopwales. co.uk. Mon–Sat 10am–5pm.

There's a great selection of Wales-themed souvenirs on offer at this friendly shop – as the name suggests, sheepy items are perhaps most prominent, but you'll also find dragons and lovespoons, and a fine array of locally produced food and drink. A perfect place to find a gift, even if only for you.

### The Window

MAP P.34

21 Charles Street, Milford Haven, SA73 2AA. 07738 152644, www. thewindowmilfordhaven.com. Mon–Sat 10am–4pm.

You'll find a fun range of ethnic products available at the Window, including such delights as clothing, rugs, jewellery, incense, soft furnishings, rugs, essential oils and candles, among much else. Many of the items on sale are hand-made. A real treasure trove!

Overlooking Broad Haven

# Restaurants

### Impasto Pizza Bar

MAP P.34

4 & 5 Sovereign House, Nelson Quay, Milford Haven, SA73 3AJ. 01646 278220, www.impasto-pizza.co.uk. Tues–Sat 5pm–9pm.

This small place on Milford Haven's waterfront serves up fantastic pizza in a great range of flavours: the Triton (£11), which comes particularly recommended, features anchovies, black olives and capers, but you won't go wrong with anything here. Vegetarians and vegans are amply catered for, and if you're not a pizza fan, there's a decent selection of pasta dishes too. The owners are planning to open a gelato parlour just along the waterfront in time for the 2022 summer season.

### Ocean Café Bar and Restaurant

MAP P.34

Enfield Road, Broad Haven, SA62 3JG. 01437 781882, www. oceancafebarandrestaurant.co.uk. Daily 9am–11pm.

Unfussy but tasty dishes await diners at the Ocean Café Bar and Restaurant, which boasts perfect views over Broad Haven's vast sandy beach – it's a great spot to watch the sunset over an evening meal. There's a lively bar too, which makes it Broad Haven's top nightlife destination.

# Cafés

### Get the Boys a Lift

MAP P.34

7A Dew Street, Haverfordwest, SA61 1ST. 01437 764983, www.facebook.com/ gettheboysalift. Mon–Fri 7.30am–4pm, Sat 9am–1pm.

Get the Boys a Lift, a not-for-profit place that does great work supporting mental health in the community, is a worthy place to get your caffeine fix – and since it's widely touted as serving the best coffee in Pembrokeshire, there really is no excuse for not stopping by when you're in town.

## Lobster & Môr

MAP P.34

Grove Place, Little Haven, SA62 3UG. 01437 781959, www.lobsterandmor.co.uk. May–Sept Tue–Sun 10am–4pm, Oct–Apr Thu–Sun 10am–4pm.

Though good coffee and tea are available, Lobster & Môr really makes waves for its deliciously fresh lobster and crab sandwiches (£9.50) – they may not be cheap, but the quality is extremely high. There's also a great range of deli products for sale, so you can stock up on local delicacies from cheese to gin.

## Runwayskiln

MAP P.34

Marloes Sands, SA62 3BH. 01646 636545, www.runwayskiln.co.uk. Hours vary by season; check the website for details.

You'll find great coffee and cakes, as well as more substantial meals, at this little place just outside the Marloes Beach car park. A stop here is perfect for refuelling after a hard day on the beach, or makes an ideal lunch stop if you're walking the coast path. The carrot cake is magnificent.

# Pubs

## The Castle

MAP P.34

1 Grove Place, Little Haven, SA62 3UG. 01437 781445, www.facebook.com/castlelittlehaven. Sun–Fri 11am–11pm, Sat 11am–midnight.

The Castle makes the most of its enviable position on Little Haven's seafront with ample outdoor seating, as well as plenty of space indoors for less sunny days. The food is reliably good, offering all the standard pub dishes spiced up with frequently changing specials.

The Griffin Inn overlooking Dale beach

## Griffin Inn

MAP P.34

Waterfront, SA62 3RB. 01646 636227, www.griffininndale.co.uk. Daily May–Sept noon–11pm, Oct–Apr hours vary – check website for details.

A lovely and friendly village pub with a great atmosphere that's won awards for its excellent fish and seafood, much of which is caught by local fishermen. The Griffin is also a great place to come just for a drink – there's a fine selection of local real ales here, and you can enjoy putting your feet up by a roaring log fire in winter.

## The Pembroke Yeoman

MAP P.34

11 Hill Street, Haverfordwest, SA61 1QQ. 01437 762500, www.facebook.com/thepembrokeyeoman. Fri–Sat 5pm–11pm, Sun noon–6pm.

Offering live music and a warm welcome, the Pembroke Yeoman is without a doubt one of the best pubs in Haverfordwest. The menu changes from month to month, but the food is never less than excellent. If you're after a drink, there's a good selection of real ales and some great cocktails.

# Pembroke and around

The county town until supplanted by Haverfordwest in 1543, Pembroke sits just inland from the southern bank of the Cleddau. It's a small town with a disproportionately large castle, which is one of the county's best and will have you exploring its towers and passages for hours. South of Pembroke, you'll find some of Pembrokeshire's finest beaches – Barafundle Bay and Broad Haven South are small and beautiful, while over to the west on the Angle peninsula is the enormous expanse of Freshwater West, backed by sand dunes and a popular destination for sun worshippers, surfers and Hollywood film crews. On the peninsula's south is Bosherston with its beautiful lily ponds, which are an ideal spot for an easy stroll or a jumping off point for the lovely coastal path around Stackpole Head.

## Pembroke

MAP P.41

Pembroke is dominated by its huge castle, but also it's worth a quick explore down the main street, which is lined with some pleasant brightly-painted shops. If you fancy a short walk, there are

Pembroke Castle

fabulous views of the castle from riverside paths – cross the bridge on Northgate Street and take the first left, heading past the Cornstore Café (see page 46).

## Pembroke Castle

MAP P.44

Westgate Hill, Pembroke, SA71 4LA. 01646 681510, www.pembrokecastle.co.uk. Daily May–Aug 9.30am–5.30pm, Sep–Oct 10am–5.30pm, Nov–Apr 10am–4pm. £7.

One of the finest fortresses in Wales, the enormous bulk of the Norman-built Pembroke Castle will keep castle enthusiasts entertained for hours. The gatehouse and adjacent towers are exceptionally well-preserved and are ideal for games of hide-and-seek, while on the other side of the courtyard you'll find the enormous cylindrical keep, from whose pinnacle there are magnificent views over the castle and town beyond. Don't miss Wogan Cavern (accessible by a staircase in the castle's Northern Hall), which is a huge, dark and slimy cave beneath the fortress: despite what your imagination may suggest, it wasn't used as a

# William Marshal

Pembroke Castle was first built by Arnulf of Montgomery in around 1093, but was remodelled in the years after 1189 by William Marshal, one of the most powerful nobles in England. From relatively humble beginnings, Marshal faithfully served no fewer than five English kings, including Richard the Lionheart, who allowed him to marry Isabel de Clare, the daughter of the Earl of Pembroke. In so doing, Marshal became the owner of Pembroke Castle, and made it a personal project to improve the fortress – much of the castle's current structure, including its impressive keep, comes from Marshal's designs.

dungeon, but rather for food and water storage, and perhaps even as a boathouse.

Pembroke Castle's history is eventful, but its greatest claim to fame is perhaps as the birthplace of Henry Tudor in 1457. Henry would eventually become king of England and found the Tudor dynasty, and is commemorated by a statue on Northgate Street below the castle, as well as by a waxwork

of him and his mother in the tower in which he was born.

## Pembroke Museum

MAP P.44

Main Street, Pembroke, SA71 4LS. 01646 683092, www.pembrokemuseum.wales. Free.

The town's museum, housed in the town hall on Main Street, walks you through Pembroke's history by way of a hodgepodge of exhibits that include a decent array of

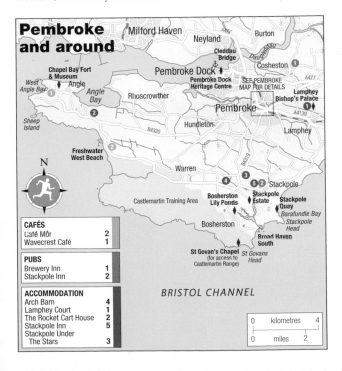

# Pembroke and around

Milford Haven
Burton
Neyland
Cleddau Bridge
Cosheston ①
Chapel Bay Fort & Museum
West Angle Bay ①
Angle
Angle Bay
Pembroke Dock
Pembroke Dock Heritage Centre
SEE PEMBROKE MAP FOR DETAILS
Lamphey Bishop's Palace ①
Sheep Island
Rhoscrowther
Pembroke ①
Lamphey
Hundleton
②
Freshwater West Beach ②
Warren
**N**
④ ③ ⑤② Stackpole
Castlemartin Training Area
Bosherston Lily Ponds
Stackpole Estate
Stackpole Quay
Barafundle Bay
Bosherston
Stackpole Head
Broad Haven South
St Govan's Chapel (for access to Castlemartin Range)
St Govans Head

*BRISTOL CHANNEL*

| CAFÉS | |
|---|---|
| Café Môr | 2 |
| Wavecrest Café | 1 |

| PUBS | |
|---|---|
| Brewery Inn | 1 |
| Stackpole Inn | 2 |

| ACCOMMODATION | |
|---|---|
| Arch Barn | 4 |
| Lamphey Court | 1 |
| The Rocket Cart House | 2 |
| Stackpole Inn | 5 |
| Stackpole Under The Stars | 3 |

| 0 | kilometres | 4 |
|---|---|---|
| 0 | miles | 2 |

national costumes and children's toys, among much else. The town hall is also home to an extensive set of large murals that tell the story of Pembroke in pictorial form. At time of research, the museum was closed due to Covid-19; check the website for the most up-to-date information.

## Pembroke Dock Heritage Centre

MAP P.41

Dockyard Chapel, Meyrick Owen Way, Pembroke Dock, SA72 6WS. 01646 684220, www.sunderlandtrust.com. Mon–Fri 10am–4pm. £5.

This extensive museum has a medley of exhibits which cheerfully, if a little haphazardly, take you through the history of Pembroke Dock, largely focussing on the two world wars. Numerous information boards tell interesting and occasionally surprising stories – for example, did you know the Millennium Falcon model for Star Wars was built here? – and there are a few fun and interactive displays that will keep the kids entertained, as well as fascinating model ships

and plenty of artefacts such as uniforms, radios, ration books and plane propellers.

## Cleddau Bridge

MAP P.41

The bridge over the Cleddau from Pembroke Dock to Neyland affords spectacular views of the boats in the river below. It's particularly attractive at sunset, when the masts of the boats and the full skies are reflected in the clear water.

## Lamphey Bishop's Palace

MAP P.41

Off the A4139, SA71 5NT. 01646 672224, www.cadw.gov.wales/visit/places-to-visit/ lamphey-bishops-palace. Daily 10am–4pm (if visitor centre is closed, enter through the side gate). Free.

A couple of miles east of Pembroke, the evocative ruins of the Bishop's Palace convey a similar sense of grandeur to those at the slightly better-preserved Palace at St Davids. Lamphey was also built by Bishop Gower and was a lucrative estate for the bishops. Hints of the Palace's former luxury can still be seen in traces of decoration in the Western

The Inner Gatehouse at Lamphey Bishop's Palace

Hall, and in the elaborate carved ceiling arches in the De Gower Hall.

## Stackpole Estate

MAP P.41
Stackpole, SA71 5DJ. 01646 661442,
www.stackpole-walled-gardens.co.uk.
Daily Apr–Oct 10am–5pm, Nov Mon–Fri
11am–3.30pm. Free.

Directly south of Pembroke, much of the coastal region is part of the Stackpole Estate, now owned by the National Trust. There used to be a country house here which sadly no longer remains, but you can visit an exhibition on the estate's history housed in the former dairy, brewery and game larder. It's also worth popping into the adjacent walled gardens.

## Stackpole Head

MAP P.41

There's some utterly fantastic coastal path walking in the region around Stackpole. Leave the car at the National Trust car park at Stackpole Quay and head south along the cliff path; after ten to fifteen minutes you'll reach Barafundle Bay, which is blessed with clear waters and soft sand, making it indisputably one of Wales' finest beaches. If you can tear yourself away, continue along the path to find yourself on Stackpole Head, a grassy promontory with magnificent views – on a clear day, you can see Caldey Island near Tenby, and even sometimes across to the Gower Peninsula. The cliff

Barafundle Bay

path will eventually lead you down to the beach at Broad Haven South, another beautiful sandy expanse that's popular with bathers and bodyboarders. Church Rock, a small jagged island, makes an excellent focal point for photos of the beach.

Continuing along the cliff path from here would bring you into the Ministry of Defence Castlemartin firing range which is in use most of the year, excluding weekends and bank holidays (check current activity on 01646 662367 or www.gov.uk/government/publications/castlemartin-firing-notice--2). It's therefore a much better idea to

## Pembrokeshire in the Movies

Given Pembrokeshire's fantastic scenery and natural beauty, it's no surprise that Hollywood has come calling more than once. Freshwater West will be particularly familiar to cinephiles: not only was it the site of a French invasion in the 2010 version of *Robin Hood* starring Russell Crowe, it was the beach to which Team Harry disapparated when escaping Malfoy Manor in *Harry Potter and the Deathly Hallows*. Elsewhere, Marloes Sands was used when Kristen Stewart starred in *Snow White and the Huntsman* in 2012, with the wicked queen's castle being superimposed onto Gateholm Island, and Pembroke Castle was used in *Me Before You*, starring Emilia Clarke and released in 2016.

either retrace your steps along the cliff path, or – if you fancy a longer walk – return via the circular route past the beautiful Bosherton Lily Ponds (see page 44). To do this, walk to the back of Broad Haven South beach and take the path, turning right when you reach the lily ponds. This circular walk is approximately five miles in total.

Whichever way you choose to return to the car park, you can reward yourself with a stop at the National Trust's Boathouse Tea Room (01646 623110, www. nationaltrust.org.uk/stackpole/features/the-boathouse-tea-room), which serves up excellent cream teas.

## Bosherton

MAP P.41

In the eighteenth century, the three artificial lakes at Bosherton were created so the owners of the Stackpole Estate could go fishing.

The calm waters of the ponds are now carpeted with lilies in the summer, resulting in an absolutely beautiful sight. There are good paths and boardwalks that circle all the lakes, making it an ideal place for an afternoon walk on a sunny day, especially since the path at the southeast corner leads down to the beach at Broad Haven South, so you can break your stroll with a cooling swim. The car park, operated by the National Trust, gets busy in summer, but there is also parking available in the village, as well as a number of tea rooms.

## Castlemartin Range

MAP P.41

The area between Broad Haven South and Freshwater West is used by the Ministry of Defence as a firing range, and as such isn't accessible to the general public most of the time. One section, however, is sometimes open,

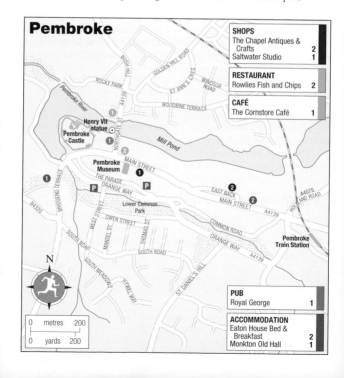

# Lord Palmerston's Follies

Many of the forts along the Pembrokeshire coast – for example, on Thorn Island at West Angle and on St Catherine's Island at Tenby – were commissioned by the 1860s Prime Minister, Lord Palmerston, who was concerned about the prospect of a French invasion, especially given the then poor state of the British navy. By the time the forts were complete in the 1880s, the threat had receded and they were never tested in combat, earning them the name of Lord Palmerston's Follies.

usually from 4.30pm onwards and at weekends, but make sure to check on www.gov.uk/government/collections/firing-notice or call 01646 662367 before you visit. It's worth checking it out if you have the opportunity: the coastline here is particularly gorgeous, especially the rock arch known as Green Bridge and the adjacent Elegug Stacks. If you do manage to make the trip, you'll park at the St Govan's Chapel car park, from which it's an easy stroll down to the eponymous chapel, a rock-hewn monastic cell that is reputedly where St Govan was miraculously saved from pirates in the sixth century.

## Freshwater West Beach

MAP P.41

Backed by towering grassy sand dunes and blessed with gorgeous rolling waves, the wide expanse of beach at Freshwater West is a perfect place to kick back and enjoy a relaxing day of sun, sand and surf. Be careful, though, as the currents here can be very strong. Stick around till the end of the day to catch a fantastic sunset looking west across the Atlantic.

## Chapel Bay Fort & Museum

MAP P.41

Angle, SA71 5BE. www.chapelbayfort.com. Fri–Sun 10am–4pm. £6.60.

Pembrokeshire's coast is peppered with nineteenth-century forts, many of which were built in anticipation of possible French invasion. The fort at Chapel Bay, just outside the village of Angle, makes a fascinating visit for history and military enthusiasts, with guided tours around the museum being led by the knowledgeable team. The on-site café isn't half bad either.

## West Angle Bay

MAP P.41

A sheltered sandy beach at the end of the Angle peninsula, this is a pleasant spot for swimming, and there are good stretches of the coastal path starting from here too – head right from the beach to find a lovely viewpoint overlooking one of Lord Palmerston's Follies, which stands on Thorn Island.

St Govan's chapel

Café Môr

# Shops

## The Chapel Antiques & Crafts

MAP P.44

East Back, Pembroke, SA71 4HL. 01646 622174, www.thechapelantiques.com. Tue–Sat 10am–5pm.

Housed in Pembroke's eighteenth-century Baptist chapel, this lovely shop is a great place to browse for new and old furniture, garden ornaments, and interior accessories. There's always a fascinating collection here, ranging from Persian rugs to rocking horses.

## Saltwater Studio

MAP P.44

25 Main St, Pembroke, SA71 4JS. 07512 261086, www.saltwaterstudiopembroke. co.uk. Tue–Sat 10am–4pm.

Marvellous craft shop in Pembroke's town centre, selling fantastic locally-made gifts including prints, ceramics, jewellery and clothing. If you're looking for a stylish souvenir of your trip to Pembrokeshire, this is a perfect place to start.

# Restaurant

## Rowlies Fish and Chips

MAP P.44

2 Main Street, Pembroke, SA71 4NP. 01646 686172. Mon–Sat 11am–8pm.

Deservedly popular place in Pembroke's town centre, dishing up great fish in crispy batter accompanied by lovely golden chips. There is a sit-in option available, but if it's a nice day consider getting takeaway and sitting down by the river with fantastic views of the castle.

# Cafés

## Café Môr

MAP P.41

Freshwater West Beach Car Park, SA71 5AH. 07422 535345, www.beachfood.co.uk/ pages/cafe-mor-menu. Daily Apr–Jun & Sep 9am–4pm, Jul–Aug 8am–4pm, Oct 9am–3pm.

The fabulous Café Môr describes itself as a "solar-powered-mobile-seaweed-kitchen" that serves "the finest beach food in the world", and it's hard to disagree. The menu includes great bacon rolls and burgers, but it really excels with the seafood – the crab and lobster rolls are utterly delicious. If you want something lighter, there's great local ice cream – including rum sorbet from Narberth's Fire and Ice shop (see page 60) – and to drink, try the seaweed tea.

## The Cornstore Café

MAP P.44

North Quay Court, The Green, Pembroke, SA71 4NQ. 01646 684290, www.facebook. com/CornstoreCafe. Mon–Sat 10am–4pm.

As the name suggests, this lovely stone and wood-beamed building was once the corn store for the mill, which was on the bridge nearby. It's now been repurposed as a fantastic café, with lovely sandwiches and great cakes. The white chocolate cheesecake (£3.50) is highly calorific but totally worth it.

## Wavecrest Café

MAP P.41
West Angle Bay, SA71 5BE. 01646 641457,
www.wavecrestangle.co.uk. Apr–Sep Mon–
Thu 10.30–4pm, Fri–Sun 10.30am–5pm,
Oct–Dec & Feb–Mar Thu–Sun 11am–4pm.
Beachside café at West Angle
Bay serving tasty lunch options,
including lovely sandwiches
and baguettes, and a delicious
cheesy garlic bread – just the
thing to warm you up after an
invigorating dip.

# Pubs

## Brewery Inn

MAP P.41
Cosheston, SA72 4UD. 01646 686678, www.
thebreweryinn.com. Tue 6pm–10pm, Wed–
Sat noon–3pm & 6pm–10pm, Sun noon–5pm.
The Brewery Inn is a welcoming
local pub in the small village of
Cosheston. The menu consists of
great local produce with a meat and
seafood focus, and there's a lovely
beer garden in which to enjoy a
drink in warm weather. If it's cold
outside, though, it's a rare treat to
hunker down in the pub's lounge
next to the wood fire stove.

## Royal George

MAP P.44
2 The Quay, Pembroke, SA71 4NT. 01646
686819, www.facebook.com/royal.george.
pembroke. Mon–Sat 11am–10pm, Sun
noon–10pm.
Nestled just below Pembroke's
castle, the Royal George offers
a hearty Welsh welcome and is
a decent place to stop for a bite
to eat while in town. The menu
includes all the traditional pub
favourites, as well as lighter lunch
options such as filling baguettes
and warming jacket potatoes with
all the toppings.

## Stackpole Inn

MAP P.41
Jasons Corner, Stackpole, SA71 5DF.
01646 672324, www.stackpoleinn.co.uk.
Mon–Sat noon–2.30pm & 5.30pm–8pm,
Sun noon–3pm.
A lovely old pub in a seventeenth-
century building, the Stackpole
serves upmarket pub food and also
has a good selection of local ales.
Make sure to check the specials
menu, as there's often some
excellent fish or seafood available.
The Sunday lunchtime roasts are
well worth making the trip for.

The Stackpole Inn garden

# Tenby and around

The southeast corner of Pembrokeshire around Tenby is one of the best areas in which to base yourself for your trip. Tenby itself is an attractive seaside resort, with a history stretching back to the medieval period but popular with tourists since the Victorian era. Here, you can relax on the sandy beach, enjoy some of the county's best cafés and restaurants, or take a boat trip across to Caldey Island. The surrounding countryside is peppered with castles and beautiful beaches, and there's a trio of excellent activities for families on the B4318 road: take your pick from Manor Wildlife Park, Heatherton World of Activities, and the Dinosaur Park.

## Tenby Museum and Art Gallery

MAP P.51
Castle Hill, Tenby, SA70 7BP. 01834 842809, www.tenbymuseum.org.uk. Thu–Sat 10am–4pm. £4.95.

The ground floor of Tenby's museum walks you through the history of the wider area, starting with Pembrokeshire's geological history. There are some great fossils on display – look out for the impressive sea snail in limestone,

St Catherine's Island

as well as an array of finds that indicate the area was once home to a fine selection of prehistoric beasts including cave lions and woolly mammoth. From the human era, there's a good overview of the Bronze and Iron Ages before the displays move on to the Roman, medieval and modern periods. The history lesson continues upstairs, focussing more on Tenby itself, with information boards and a range of exhibits spanning the centuries – check out the magnificent penny farthing bike.

The building is also home to an art gallery which concentrates primarily on local artists, with Augustus John – born in Tenby in 1878 – taking pride of place. Rock music fans may wish to keep their eyes peeled for the work by Nicky Wire of the Manic Street Preachers, whose solo art show was exhibited here in 2018.

## Castle Hill

MAP P.51

There's not a lot left of the medieval fortress that once stood on this site – just a fairly small tower that's now rather overshadowed by the adjacent memorial to Prince Albert, Queen Victoria's consort. Perhaps the most compelling reason to come up here is for the fantastic views across town and to

St Catherine's Island nearby. At the bottom of the hill, on Harbour Square, you'll see the Sea Water Baths and Assembly Rooms, which were built by Sir William Paxton in the early nineteenth century as part of an effort to attract tourists to the town.

## Beaches

MAP P.51

Tenby is blessed with several beaches, the most obvious of which is North Beach, a fantastic curve of sand that sweeps around the bay from the Park Hotel at the north end of town to Castle Hill. Right in the middle of North Beach is a craggy outcrop known as Goskar Rock, which is the beach's central feature. On the other side of Castle Hill is Castle Beach, a small and usually fairly quiet expanse of sand, which is dominated by a view of St Catherine's Island and its 1869 fort. Finally, on the town's south side

is the aptly named South Beach, a long and sandy expanse backed by dunes that's normally busiest at the northeast end, closest to town.

## Tudor Merchant's House

MAP P.51
Quay Hill, Tenby, SA70 7BX. 01834 842279, www.nationaltrust.org.uk/ tudor-merchants-house. Apr–Oct daily 11am–5pm. £6.

In the late fifteenth century, Tenby was second only to Bristol as a west-coast port, and many inhabitants of the town became rich from trade in a variety of goods, including cloth, coal, vinegar and spices. The Tudor Merchant's House is where one such trader lived: its three floors have been furnished with both reproduction and original decorations and items, which help to bring to life the domestic arrangements of a family from this period. The herb garden at the

Caldey Abbey

## Caldey Island

MAP P.49
Two miles offshore. 01834 844453, www.
caldeyislandwales.com. Access is by boat
from Tenby Harbour (or Castle Beach when
the tide is out) every 20min (Easter–Oct
Mon–Fri, May–Sept Mon–Sat, 10am–5pm;
20min each way). £12 return.

Caldey Island was settled by Celtic
monks in the sixth century, but
this initial community was most
likely wiped out by Viking raids.
In 1136, however, the Benedictine
monks of St Dogmael's near
Cardigan founded a priory here,
which lasted until the dissolution
of the monasteries in 1536. Since
1906, the island has again been a
monastic home, with fifteen monks
currently in residence, alongside
a colony of red squirrels that were
reintroduced in 2016.

From the island's jetty a short
woodland walk leads to its main
settlement: a tiny post office,
the popular tea gardens and a
perfume shop selling the herbal
fragrances distilled from Caldey's
abundant flora by the monks. A
lane leads south from the village
to the old priory, abandoned in
1536 and restored after 1897. Its
centrepiece is the twelfth-century
St Illtud's church, distinguished
by the presence of one of the most
significant pre-Norman finds in
Wales: the Ogham Stone. This was
discovered under the stained-glass
window on the south side of the
nave, and bears a runic inscription
from the sixth century (added to, in
Latin, during the ninth). From the
priory, the lane continues south,
climbing up to the gleaming white
lighthouse, built in 1828 – views
from here are memorable.

## Saundersfoot

MAP P.49
Three miles north of Tenby,
Saundersfoot is a lively little village
which was built in the nineteenth
century off the back of the local
anthracite coal industry. It has a
great beach and attractive harbour,

back gives a good view of the huge
Flemish chimney.

## St Mary's church

MAP P.51
Between Tudor Square and St George's St,
Tenby, SA70 8AP. Usually open. Free.

The town centre's focal point
is the 152ft spire of the largely
fifteenth-century St Mary's church.
Venture inside to check out the
elaborate carvings on the chancel
ceiling and the tombs of various
local merchants. Also on show here
is a tablet memorialising the Tudor
mathematician Richard Recorde,
who was born in Tenby around
1510 and was the inventor of the
"equals" symbol.

## Town walls

MAP P.51
South Parade, Tenby, SA70 7DL. 24h. Free.

A good stretch of Tenby's medieval
town walls are still standing, and can
be best seen with a short amble along
South Parade and St Florence Parade.
The Five Arches Tower, once one of
the only two entrances into the walled
town, is particularly worth a look –
true to its name, it has five arches, and
as such is rather distinctive.

but where it really punches above its weight is in its proliferation of boutique shops and fine dining options. If you're seeking a bit of an adrenaline rush, consider booking a water-based activity with Outer Reef such as surfing, coasteering or paddleboarding.

## Kilgetty Ironworks
MAP P.49

Those interested in Pembrokeshire's industrial heritage may want to make a short stop off at the hulking ruins of Kilgetty's ironworks, which were established in the 1840s but never appear to have been hugely successful, and were closed down only thirty years later in 1877. A path leads up behind the ironworks allowing access to further remains.

## Colby Woodland Garden
MAP P.49
Near Amroth, SA67 8PP. 01834 811885, www.nationaltrust.org.uk/colby-woodland-garden. Daily 10am–5pm; walled garden summer months only. Free; parking charges apply (£3 for three hours).

Offering essentially what it says on the tin, Colby Woodland Garden consists of a formal wooded landscape, with a walled garden and a wider estate criss-crossed with waymarked trails. It's a perfectly pleasant place for a walk, though it rather lacks the drama of the coastal path.

## Amroth
MAP P.49

Amroth, site of the southern beginning or end of the Pembrokeshire Coastal Path – depending on which way you're walking – boasts an excellent wide sandy beach. It's also got something of an industrial history – high quality Welsh anthracite coal was mined here, and a seam of it can still be seen in the cliff at the east end of the beach.

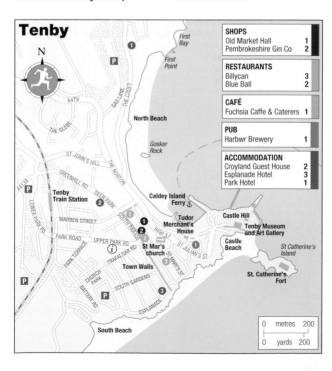

**Tenby**

| SHOPS | |
|---|---|
| Old Market Hall | 1 |
| Pembrokeshire Gin Co | 2 |

| RESTAURANTS | |
|---|---|
| Billycan | 3 |
| Blue Ball | 2 |

| CAFÉ | |
|---|---|
| Fuchsia Caffe & Caterers | 1 |

| PUB | |
|---|---|
| Harbwr Brewery | 1 |

| ACCOMMODATION | |
|---|---|
| Croyland Guest House | 2 |
| Esplanade Hotel | 3 |
| Park Hotel | 1 |

First Bay
First Point
North Beach
Gosker Rock
Tenby Train Station
WARREN STREET
PARK ROAD
Caldey Island Ferry
Tudor Merchant's House
Castle Hill
Tenby Museum and Art Gallery
Castle Beach
St Mary's church
Town Walls
St Catherine's Island
St. Catherine's Fort
ESPLANADE
South Beach

0 metres 200
0 yards 200

## Dinosaur Park

MAP P.49

B4318, near Tenby, SA70 8RB. 01834 845272, www.thedinosaurpark.co.uk. Daily May–Sep 10am–5pm, Oct 10.30am–4pm. £14.95.

Kids will love the dino-themed entertainments on offer at the excellent Dinosaur Park. Start off by following the woodland trail, which is inhabited by life-size dinosaur models that roar intimidatingly, then ramp up the adrenaline with boat, car or tube rides, and finish off with a round of dinosaur-themed crazy golf or chill out at DinoFest, where animatronic dinosaurs play drums and guitar. The place has a fantastic sense of humour which makes it a perfect afternoon out for kids and adults alike.

## Heatherton World of Activities

MAP P.49

B4318, near Tenby, SA70 8RJ. 01646 652000, www.heatherton.co.uk. Daily Apr–Jun & Sep–Oct 10am–5pm, Jul–Aug 10am–6pm, Nov–Mar 10am–4.30pm. Free entry; activities charged separately.

Crazy golf at Heatherton World of Activities

Heatherton World of Activities offers a seemingly endless range of diversions to keep the kids (and grown-ups!) busy, from go-karting to adventure golf, by way of a hedge maze and zorbing. The site is also home to Pembrokeshire's first escape rooms. All activities are charged individually, so it's probably a good idea to buy a set number of credits, depending on how many things you want to do.

## Manor Wildlife Park

MAP P.49

B4318, near Tenby, SA70 8RJ. 01646 651201, www.manorwildlifepark.co.uk. Daily Apr–Oct 10am–5pm, Nov–Mar 10am–4pm. £17.95.

There's a fine collection of animals at Manor Wildlife Park, from favourites such as rhinos and gibbons through to red pandas and wallabies. Animal encounters are available – who could resist the opportunity to feed the tigers? – and it's possible for both adults and children to experience what it's like to be a keeper for the day. If the kids need to run off some steam, there's also an extensive indoor play area.

## Carew Castle and Tidal Mill

MAP P.49

Castle Ln, Carew, SA70 8SL. 01646 651782, www.pembrokeshirecoast.wales/ carew-castle. Castle & mill daily Apr–Oct 10am–5pm; castle only Nov–Mar Mon–Fri 11am–3pm. £5.50.

Carew Castle, situated on the banks of the Cleddau river, is a fine example of a medieval fortress that grew over time into more of a Tudor country estate: the defensive towers of the original castle merge seamlessly into the fine mansion-like range of the Elizabethan extension. There's a good run-through of the castle's history in the undercroft, and you'll also find info boards dotted around detailing some of the castle's more interesting inhabitants, including a flamboyant Elizabethan noble called John Perrot, who was rumoured to be an illegitimate son of Henry VIII, and the unfortunate Sir Roland Rhys, who was killed by his pet ape in the North West Tower. Note the coats of arms above the entranceway to the Great Hall – these are the heraldic logos of Henry VII, his son Arthur, and Catherine of Aragon.

A short walk around the mill pond brings you to the imposing Tidal Mill, which was probably established in the sixteenth century, but was rebuilt in 1800 and last used in 1937. Inside, you can view the mill's machinery and learn how water was used to generate power.

## Manorbier Castle

MAP P.49

Manorbier, SA70 7SY. 01834 870081, www. manorbiercastle.co.uk. Daily Apr–Oct 10am–4pm. £5.50.

About six miles west of Tenby is the small village of Manorbier and its well-preserved medieval castle. With fine views from the battlements, a warren of dark passageways to explore, and a pleasant central green lawn and gardens, it's a great place for history buffs. In one room, you'll find a waxwork of Gerald of Wales, a twelfth-century churchman and writer whose sadly never-realised ambition

was to become Bishop of St Davids. Children of the 80s might recognise Manorbier Castle as the filming location for Cair Paravel in the BBC's adaptation of *The Lion, the Witch and the Wardrobe*.

## Manorbier Beach

MAP P.49

Surrounded by striking red sandstone rocks, and overlooked by the brooding presence of the castle, Manorbier's small sand and pebble beach is an attractive place for a swim. There's good coastal path walking from here too: in particular, make sure you wander up the cliff path heading south from the beach for about ten minutes to come across the King's Quoit, a Neolithic burial chamber.

## Church Door Cove

MAP P.49

If you're walking the cliff path in the area between Manorbier and Tenby, it's definitely worth making a quick detour down the steep steps to Church Door Cove. Here, the almighty power of the sea has eroded the cliff into a perfectly square arch, and it's fantastic to sit on the beach and watch the waves crash through the passage. Though it's accessible at any time of day, the beach is at its best at low tide, when there's a fine stretch of golden sand visible.

## Gerald of Wales

Born at Manorbier Castle in the mid twelfth century, Gerald of Wales was a prolific writer who produced two works entitled *The Journey Through Wales* and *The Description of Wales*, which act as early guidebooks, describing the beauty of the country and recommending places to visit. Possibly biased, he considered that "in all the broad lands of Wales, Manorbier is the most pleasant place by far". Despite his sobriquet and his at least one-quarter Welsh heritage, Gerald considered himself a Norman, and was relentlessly rude about the native Welsh in his works, though he did concede that although "you may never find anyone worse than a bad Welshman, you will certainly never find anyone better than a good one."

# Shops

## Chobbles Sweet Shop

MAP P.49
Kensington House, The Strand,
Saundersfoot, SA69 9ET. 01834 810210,
www.chobbles.com. Daily 10am–6pm.
Those with a sweet tooth will be
in seventh heaven in this great
traditional sweet shop that stocks a
veritable cornucopia of sweets and
chocolates. There's a very fine selection
of fudge too – the sea salt caramel is
the absolute pick of the bunch, but
the Jamaican rum is a close second.

## Old Market Hall

MAP P.51
High St, Tenby, SA70 7EU. Daily 10am–5pm.
Tenby's Victorian Market Hall is
worth a wander – there are plenty
of little shops in here, including
an excellent deli, a spot selling
great photos of Tenby and the
surrounding area, and a Malaysian
street food stall that infuses the
whole place with a delicious aroma.

## Pembrokeshire Gin Co

MAP P.51
Upper Frog St, Tenby, SA70 7JD. www.

Pembrokeshire Gin Co

pembsginco.co.uk. Mon–Sat 10am–5pm,
Sun 10am–4pm.
The Pembrokeshire Gin Co began
operations in 2018 and has quickly
established an excellent reputation;
their gins have won several national
awards. There are three different
varieties, of which the slightly
spicy Welshcake gin is especially
delicious. There are also gin glasses
and tonic on sale, as well as a small
selection of Pembrokeshire Gin
Company merchandise.

# Restaurants

## Billycan

MAP P.51
Lower Frog St, Tenby, SA70 7HS. 01834
842172, www.billycan-tenby.co.uk. Mon–
Thu noon–11.30pm (Tue closed in winter),
Fri–Sat noon–midnight, Sun noon–11pm.
This stylish place serves up a
crowd-pleasing selection of good
solid meals, with a great range of
burgers, steaks and fish options.
The Sunday roast dinners always
prove extremely popular.

## Blue Ball

MAP P.51
10 Upper Frog St, Tenby, SA70 7JD. 01834
843038, www.blueballtenby.com. Tue–Sat
5pm–10pm.
This atmospheric place with a beautiful
wood-beamed ceiling serves excellent
British and Welsh fare, offering some
fantastic meat and seafood dishes.
The belly pork (£18.50) is absolutely
sublime. Advance booking is highly
recommended.

## Coast

MAP P.49
Coppet Hall Beach, Saundersfoot, SA69 9AJ.
01834 826100, www.coastsaundersfoot.
co.uk. Wed 6.30pm–8.30pm, Thu–Sun
noon–2pm & 6.30pm–8.30pm.
If you're looking to splash out,
the seasonal cuisine at Coast is an
excellent choice. Enjoy the tasting
menu (£65pp) from the elegant
restaurant overlooking the sea for a
truly refined evening.

## Dragon Palace

MAP P.49

Pentlepoir, Saundersfoot, SA69 9BH. 01834 812483, www.dragon-palace.co.uk. Daily noon–2pm & 5pm–10pm.

This award-winning restaurant serves up some of the best Chinese food you'll find in Pembrokeshire. There's a lot on the menu, but if you're after recommendations, the crispy duck pancakes are perfect and the Kung Po chicken is excellent. It's a popular place, so it's a good idea to book in advance. Also does takeaway and delivery.

# Cafés

## Beach Break Tearooms

MAP P.49

Manorbier House, Manorbier, SA70 7TD. 01834 871709, www.facebook.com/beachbreaktearooms. Daily Feb–Oct 10am–4pm.

Popular café in Manorbier village that serves up great breakfasts and lunches, but perhaps the real draw is the excellent selection of homemade cakes. Make sure to browse the nearby gift shop too, both for souvenirs and further edible treats.

## Fuchsia Caffe & Caterers

MAP P.51

The Mews, Upper Frog Street, Tenby, SA70 7JD. 01834 219224, www.thefuchsiacaffe.co.uk/home. Tue–Sat 9am–5pm, Sun 9am–3pm.

Set in a small quiet courtyard, Fuchsia is a pleasant little spot that's ideal for a light lunch. The Welsh rarebit (£7.50) comes particularly recommended.

## Pirate Café

MAP P.49

Amroth seafront, SA67 8NF. 01834 812757. Fri–Tue 9.30am–4pm.

Just opposite Amroth's beach, the Pirate Café is the perfect spot for lunch, coffee, cake or ice cream, either sit-in or takeaway. There's a gift shop attached too, so if you're in need of a souvenir or a bucket and spade, this is the place to be.

The Pirate Cafe

# Pubs

## The Carew Inn

MAP P.49

Bird's Lane, Carew, SA70 8SL. 01646 651267, www.carewinn.co.uk. Daily noon–11pm.

Just across the road from the castle, the Carew Inn is a lively and friendly pub that serves great bar food and offers a fine selection of real ales. For hot summer days there's a lovely beer garden in which to kick back and enjoy a pint (or two), and in the winter the pub is warmed by an open fire. A real gem.

## Harbwr Brewery

MAP P.51

Sergeants Lane, SA70 7BU. 01834 845797, www.harbwr.wales. Daily 10.30am–10pm.

Housed in a marvellously atmospheric eighteenth-century warehouse on an alley behind the Tudor Merchant's House, Harbwr Brewery's taproom serves a wide range of Harbwr beers, from pale ale to stout, as well as a very good selection of gins and guest real ales. There's a second, equally good, branch in Saundersfoot.

# Narberth and around

The town of Narberth is sometimes referred to as the capital of the Landsker Borderlands: 'landsker' is a Norse word meaning 'frontier', and it's roughly here that Pembrokeshire divides between the Welsh-speaking north and the anglicised south, a division that's existed since the Norman period. Narberth is a lovely little town with a fantastic museum and some of Pembrokeshire's finest dining and shopping options, and the surrounding region is dotted with castles and stately homes. Not only that but you'll also find some great options for adrenaline junkies, including Oakwood theme park and the Wild Lakes activity centre, or family days out such as Picton Castle and Folly Farm. It's an often overlooked part of the county that deserves exploration.

## Narberth Museum

MAP P.57

The Bonded Stores, Church Street, Narberth SA67 7BH. 01834 860500, www.narberthmuseum.co.uk. Tue–Sat 10am–5pm. £4.50.

The excellent Narberth Museum is housed in the former Bonded Stores, where alcohol – notably Scottish and Irish whiskies – was brought for storage and blending. The museum gives an accordingly spirited overview of the building's past, as well as offering a wider view of Narberth's history, taking in the local wool production industry, the Rebecca Riots of the 1840s, and the arrival of the railway in 1866, among much else. Interactive exhibits – such as a medieval Welsh uprising computer game and the chance to design your own spirit bottle label – will keep the kids engaged.

## Narberth Castle

MAP P.57

Castle Terrace, Narberth, SA67 7BD. www. visitpembrokeshire.com/attraction-listing/narberth-castle. 24h. Free.

Accessed via an unlabelled gate on Castle Terrace, the fairly sparse ruins of Narberth Castle – which are identified in the great Welsh epic, the *Mabinogion*, as the court

## The Rebecca Riots

The economic position of Welsh farmers in the 1830s was generally poor, thanks to several years of substandard harvests coupled with increasing taxation. By 1842, the situation had erupted into civil unrest directed at one of the most obvious targets: toll gates on main roads that exacted taxes for farmers taking goods to market. Taking inspiration from the biblical character of Rebecca – who, in Genesis, stated her intention to "possess the gates of those that hate them" – male rioters frequently dressed in women's clothing and destroyed tollgates across Pembrokeshire and Carmarthenshire. An increased troop presence in the area led to the decline of the Rebecca movement, and the riots ended in 1843. The following year the Turnpikes Act was passed, which halved the toll rates.

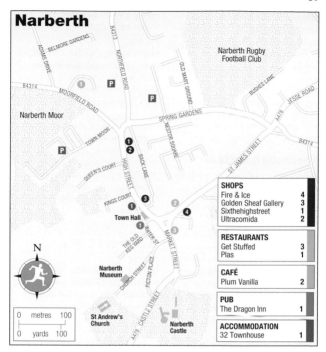

# Narberth

**SHOPS**
| | |
|---|---|
| Fire & Ice | 4 |
| Golden Sheaf Gallery | 3 |
| Sixthighstreet | 1 |
| Ultracomida | 2 |

**RESTAURANTS**
| | |
|---|---|
| Get Stuffed | 3 |
| Plas | 1 |

**CAFÉ**
| | |
|---|---|
| Plum Vanilla | 2 |

**PUB**
| | |
|---|---|
| The Dragon Inn | 1 |

**ACCOMMODATION**
| | |
|---|---|
| 32 Townhouse | 1 |

of Pwyll, Prince of Dyfed – are worth a quick visit. A couple of information boards help you to visualise everyday life in the castle.

## Town Hall

MAP P.57

High St, Narberth, SA67 7AR. 01834 860407, www.goldensheafgallery.co.uk. Mon–Sat 10am–5pm. Free.

A tall and thin building that rather resembles a church, Narberth Town Hall is now home to part of the Golden Sheaf Gallery (see page 60). The lower floor is thought to be the cell where the leaders of the Rebecca Riots were imprisoned.

## Oakwood Theme Park

MAP P.58

Canaston Bridge, Narberth SA67 8DE. 01834 815170, www.oakwoodthemepark. co.uk. May–Jun Fri–Mon 10am–4.30pm, early Jul Wed–Mon 10am–5pm, late Jul–Aug Wed–Mon 10am–8pm, Sep–Oct Sat–Sun 10am–4.30pm. £33.50.

Wales' largest theme park makes for a fine day out for thrill-seekers, with adrenaline-boosting rides such as the enormous wooden rollercoaster *Megafobia*, the tidal-wave-producing *Drenched*, and *Speed*, which more than lives up to its name. There's also plenty to entertain those who don't wish their heart rate to hit the danger zone, including the bobsleigh, the *Treetops* rollercoaster and *Snake River Falls*. For younger visitors, the Peter Pan-themed Neverland section offers great family rides.

## Wild Lakes

MAP P.58

Cott Lane, Martletwy, SA67 8AB. 01834 891511, www.wildlakeswales.com. Mon noon–6pm, Tue 10am–6pm, Wed–Sat 10am–8pm, Sun 10am–6pm (some activities are unavailable in winter). Free entry; activities charged separately.

The Wild Lakes centre is a great place to get active on the water. The principal activity offered here is wakeboarding, with sessions available for beginners and those with more experience, but there are plenty of other options, including ringo rides and a water-based inflatable playground. For those who prefer dry land, there's also a bouldering and climbing wall. Also on site is the excellent Wild Lakes café/bar (see page 61).

## The Eastern Cleddau

MAP P.58

The area on the east banks of the Cleddau is a sparsely populated part of the county. Around Minwear, there are attractive wooded trails, and a little further south is the Cwm Deri vineyard, where you can enjoy wine tasting sessions and afternoon teas. It's also worth paying a visit to Lawrenny Quay, on the banks of the Cleddau, from which there's a lovely three-mile loop walk through the woods.

## Folly Farm Adventure Park and Zoo

MAP P.58

Begelly, Kilgetty, SA68 0XA. 01834 812731, www.folly-farm.co.uk. Daily May–Sep 10am–5pm, Oct & Mar–Apr 10am–4pm, Nov–Feb Sat–Sun 10am–4pm. £19.95.

Folly Farm is a petting farm, zoo, and theme park all rolled into one, so there's guaranteed to be something to entertain the whole family. The zoo is home to lions, giraffes, penguins and crocodiles, while the farm offers the chance to meet goats, donkeys, rabbits and pigs. The theme park emulates funfairs of yesteryear, with great vintage rides such as dodgems, a ghost train, and a big wheel.

## Llawhaden Castle

MAP P.58

Tal-Y-Bont Hill, Llawhaden, SA67 8HL. www.cadw.gov.wales/visit/places-to-visit/llawhaden-castle. Daily 10am–4pm. Free.

Though now largely ruined, it's easy to imagine how impressive

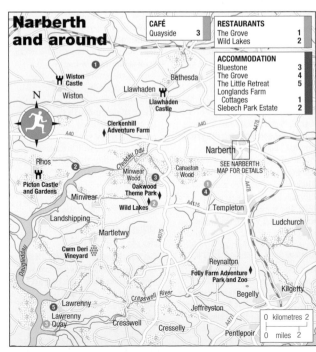

| CAFÉ | |
|---|---|
| Quayside | 3 |

| RESTAURANTS | |
|---|---|
| The Grove | 1 |
| Wild Lakes | 2 |

| ACCOMMODATION | |
|---|---|
| Bluestone | 3 |
| The Grove | 4 |
| The Little Retreat | 5 |
| Longlands Farm Cottages | 1 |
| Slebech Park Estate | 2 |

# The Mabinogion

The *Mabinogion* is the name given to a collection of stories written in Welsh in the medieval period, most likely in the twelfth century, though probably compiled from earlier writings and oral tradition. The tales include mythological epics involving princes and princesses, monsters and magicians, and the surprising appearance of some pigs from an alternate dimension. The character linking all the stories together is Pryderi, King of Dyfed, who suffers a fair number of misfortunes throughout his life before eventually losing in single combat to his enemy, Gwydion. The *Mabinogion*'s tales have been studied extensively as important medieval literature, and they have also served as inspiration for numerous writers, including JRR Tolkien and Alan Garner.

Llawhaden must have been when it was in its prime. Built by the bishops of St Davids, its half-collapsed gatehouse is still imposing; don't forget to check out the unusual and rather pleasing hexagonal Chapel and Closet Towers.

## Clerkenhill Adventure Farm

MAP P.58
Clerkenhill, SA62 4PE. 01437 751227, www.clerkenhill.co.uk. Daily Apr–Aug 10am–5pm, Sep–Oct Sat–Sun 10am–5pm. £8.50.
Clerkenhill offers a range of entertaining diversions for families, including the chance to visit the farm's animals, as well as run off some steam on the adventure playground and the go-karts. It's also blessed with an 18-hole Frizbee Golf course for the more competitively-inclined.

## Wiston Castle

MAP P.58
Wiston, SA62 4PN. www.cadw.gov.wales/visit/places-to-visit/wiston-castle. Daily 10am–4pm (officially, though can be accessed 24h). Free.
There can be few better places to see a real life example of a motte and bailey castle than Wiston. Built by a Flemish mercenary named Wizo in the early twelfth century, the earthworks surrounding the bailey can still be clearly seen, and the mound at the centre – with the remains of the stone keep still crowning its summit – is a textbook motte.

## Picton Castle

MAP P.58
Near Rhos, Haverfordwest, SA62 4AS. 01437 751326, www.pictoncastle.co.uk. Daily Apr–Oct 10am–5pm, Nov–Mar 10am–4pm. £9.
Originally a medieval fortress, Picton Castle was converted into a stately home in the eighteenth century. Visitors can explore its rooms and extensive grounds, which include a beautiful walled garden, a small zoo, and a museum featuring a collection of vintage lawnmowers. Don't miss the bird of prey demonstrations on the lawn.

Dodgems at Folly Farm

The Golden Sheaf Gallery

# Shops

### Fire & Ice
MAP P.57

66 St James St, Narberth, SA67 7DB. 01834 861995, www.fireandicewales.co.uk. Mon–Sat 10am–4.30pm.

The award-winning Fire & Ice has spotted a lucrative gap in the market: alcoholic ice cream. The cider sorbet is particularly outstanding. It's also a perfect place to stock up on non-alcoholic ice cream or non-ice-cream-ic alcohol; there is an excellent range of local craft beers and ciders, as well as Welsh gins and whiskies.

### Golden Sheaf Gallery
MAP P.57

25 High St, Narberth, SA67 7AR. 01834 860407, www.goldensheafgallery.co.uk. Mon–Sat 10am–5pm.

Housed in a Georgian town house on Narberth's main street, the Golden Sheaf Gallery is a great shop selling all manner of goods, from artwork to clothing and homeware to jewellery. It's expanded into the town hall opposite, so make sure you browse both outlets.

### Sixthehighstreet
MAP P.57

6 High St, Narberth, SA67 7AR. 01834 861063, www.sixthehighstreet.co.uk. Mon–Sat 10am–5pm.

A wide range of homeware, clothing and greeting cards, among much else, are found in this store housed in an eighteenth-century former bakery. It's also home to the Fforc deli, which offers excellent coffee and cakes, as well as more substantial edible goods for takeaway. There are plans for Fforc to move into larger premises nearby, at which point they will serve light meals too.

### Ultracomida
MAP P.57

7 High St, Narberth, SA67 7AR. 01834 861491, www.ultracomida.co.uk. Mon–Sat 11.30am–5pm.

This absolutely sublime deli specialises in all things Spanish, with a remarkable array of products ranging from cured meats, fish, cheese and olives to wine, sherry and brandy. It's pretty much impossible to enter Ultracomida without instantly spotting something you want to eat. There's a small restaurant attached, which is open for excellent meals at lunchtime.

# Restaurants

### Get Stuffed
MAP P.57

8 & 9 Market St, Narberth, SA67 7AU. 01834 860070, www.getstuffedpizza.com. Daily 5pm–10pm.

A cheap and cheerful pizza and pasta place in Narberth's town centre, this is an ideal spot if you fancy something easy either for eat-in or takeaway. There's a huge range of pizza toppings to choose from, so there's bound to be something to suit everyone's tastes.

### The Grove
MAP P.58

Molleston, Narberth, SA67 8BX. 01834 860 915, www.thegrove-narberth.co.uk/dining. Tue–Sat 6.30pm–9pm.

One of Pembrokeshire's top fine dining experiences, enjoying the tasting menu at the Fernery Restaurant in the Grove hotel is a lovely upmarket evening out. You won't come away with a lot of change, but the inventive food served, much of it grown on-site, is excellent, and is complemented by perfect wine pairings. The Artisan Rooms, also at the Grove, offer a more casual but equally delicious experience.

### Plas

MAP P.57

**Moorfield Road, Narberth, SA67 7AB. 01834 869006, www.plashyfrydhotel.com/eat-drink. Daily 5.30pm–8.30pm.**
The restaurant of the Plas Hotel offers a diverse menu: the tasty tapas choices include whitebait, Mediterranean vegetables, Asian slaw salad and mac 'n' cheese, or you could go for a "bowl" meal such as sticky sesame chicken. The adjacent bar is a lovely spot for a nightcap.

### Wild Lakes

MAP P.58

**Cott Lane, Martletwy, SA67 8AB. 01834 891511, www.wildlakeswales.com/cafe-bar. Wed–Sat noon–8pm, Sun noon–6pm.**
A venue with a difference – this place at the Wild Lakes centre is housed in a large tipi. It has a lovely convivial atmosphere, with a chilled soundtrack on the stereo and a young and hip clientele. The food is good too: there's burgers and pizzas as well as more international options such as chicken satay and Mexican pork wraps.

# Cafés

### Quayside

MAP P.58

**Lawrenny Quay, SA68 0PR. 01646 651574, www.quaysidelawrenny.co.uk. Easter–Sep Wed–Sun 11am–4pm.**
The menu at Quayside revolves mostly around seafood, with frequently changing specials that might include lobster or crab, as well as excellent regular options

Steak at Wild Lakes

such as sandwiches, baguettes and cakes. There's a lovely exterior seating area which provides a great view of the passing yachts.

### Plum Vanilla

MAP P.57

**2A St James St, Narberth, SA67 7DB. 01834 862762. Mon–Sat 9am–5pm.**
The very popular Plum Vanilla serves homemade organic food with plenty of vegetarian choices; options include the soup of the day, ciabattas, jacket potatoes and salads, and hot dishes such as tagines and red dragon pie. There's also a great deli if you'd prefer to shop for picnic supplies.

# Pubs

### The Dragon Inn

MAP P.57

**Water St, Narberth SA67 7AT. 01834 860257, www.facebook.com/thedragonnarberth. Mon–Sat 11am–10pm, Sun noon–10pm.**
This welcoming pub in Narberth's town centre is a friendly place for a pint, and the kitchen offers up decent pub grub; the Sunday roasts are very good, and the burgers are deservedly popular.

# Fishguard and around

Pembrokeshire's north coast centres around Fishguard, a small town on the mouth of the River Gwaum that is likely to have been established in the mid- to late tenth century. Its key historical moment came in 1797, when it became the site of the last invasion of mainland Britain, though now it's a pleasant, low-key and arty place that's generally noted only for being a point of departure for ferries to Ireland. The surrounding region offers some fine coastal walks; the section around Strumble Head is one of the most scenic in Pembrokeshire, and there's a short stroll from the village Abercastle which provides access to one of the county's most impressive Neolithic burial chambers.

## Last Invasion Gallery

MAP P.65
Town Hall, Market Square, Fishguard, SA65 9HE. 01437 776638, www. lastinvasiontapestry.co.uk. Mon–Wed & Fri 10am–5pm, Thu 10am–6pm, Sat 10am–4pm (until 1pm Oct–Mar). Free.

On the upper floor of Fishguard's handsome green town hall, you'll find the Last Invasion Gallery, a conscious imitation of the Bayeux Tapestry that depicts the events of the 1797 French invasion. Embroidered to mark the 200th anniversary of the invasion, the tapestry includes plenty of excellent details – look out in particular for the section depicting Jemima, a redoubtable Welshwoman who single-handedly captured twelve French soldiers, all of whom look appropriately shamefaced.

## Lower Town

MAP P.65
Fishguard's Lower Town, centred around the harbour, is a quiet and attractive place for a stroll. It's also a fine venue for crabbing if you happen to have some raw bacon about your person. The harbour – which enjoyed a moment of glory

## The Last Invasion

Now famous as the last occasion on which a foreign force invaded Britain, the French force that landed at Carregwastad Point, just north of Fishguard, in 1797 was something of a farce from the beginning. The roughly 1,400 French troops, led by the Irish-American Colonel William Tate, apparently had the expectation that the allegedly oppressed local populace would welcome them as liberators; it's unlikely that this would have proved the case, but the invasion never even got that far; the French force instead happened upon a large quantity of food and drink stashed at Trehowel Farm for an upcoming wedding, and within a very short time were too drunk and full to do anything of consequence. Within two days, the invaders had surrendered to a local militia at Fishguard's Royal Oak pub, and were taken off to imprisonment in Haverfordwest, Pembroke and Portsmouth.

in 1971, when Richard Burton and Elizabeth Taylor filmed Dylan Thomas' *Under Milk Wood* here – is home to a couple of sculptures: just outside the car park is the herring sculpture, which commemorates the town's historic herring industry, while at the opposite end of Quay Street is the Mesoamerican-influenced *Sun Lover* by local artist John Cleal.

## Fishguard Fort

MAP P.65

The ruins of Fishguard's fort stand on a promontory just north of the lower town. Not much of the fort itself remains, but it's a good spot for panoramic views back to the harbour and across east to Dinas Head.

## Dyffryn Fernant Garden

MAP P.65

Near Dinas, Fishguard, SA65 9SP. 01348 811282, www.dyffrynfernant.co.uk. Daily Apr–Oct noon–5pm. £7.

Just three miles to the east of Fishguard's, the charming gardens of Dyffryn Fernant feel truly remote. They're at their best in the spring, when they bloom into a riot of colour, but they remain well worth visiting throughout the summer and into early autumn. Visitors are welcome to explore the grounds to their fullest extent, from the Magic Garden to Hopeful Wood and everything in between, or borrow a book from the on-site library – comprised mostly of gardening and nature volumes – and enjoy it in the garden.

## Sea Môr Aquarium

MAP P.65

The Parrog, Goodwick, SA64 0DE. 01348 874737, www.seatrust.org.uk/sea-mor-aquarium. Mar–Oct Thu–Sun 10am–4.30pm (hours may be extended during holidays; check website for details). £6.50.

This small but engaging aquarium is found on the seafront in Goodwick, not far from the Irish ferry terminal. Visitors are guided round on a tour delivered by knowledgeable staff, with the opportunity to see – and sometimes touch – the marine life native to this part of Wales. The occupants of the aquarium vary as out of season most creatures are returned to the sea, but you're likely to see moon jellyfish, anemones, starfish and perhaps even an octopus.

## Strumble Head

MAP P.65

The coastal path around Strumble Head – the promontory just west of Fishguard – is one of the loveliest stretches in the county. At the northern end is the lighthouse, which is inaccessible to the public but can still be seen from the cliff path, while on the west side is the peninsula's highest point, the hulking crag of Garn Fawr, which was once an Iron Age hill fort. Climb this for fantastic views which take in pretty much the entirety of Pembrokeshire's north coast. It's particularly fine on a sunny evening, when the sunset turns the water beneath the distinctive humps of St David's Head a beautiful orange. Park by the YHA Pwll Deri (see page

Sunset at Fishguard

# Out and back walk to Carregwastad Point

Carregwastad Point, towards the eastern end of Strumble Head, was the landing place of the French invasion force in 1797, and it now makes a good destination for a short walk from Llanwnda village, about three miles out of Fishguard. If it's been wet lately, this route can be very muddy – walking boots are advised.

Before setting off from Llanwnda, take a quick look at the attractive St Gwyndaf Church, which occupies a very fine piece of real estate with great views out to sea. Then follow the path down from the church and take the waymarked path pointing left at Ysbryd Y Craig. The track then bends right after about 100m, again following a waymark, after which the route heads across well-signed fields. After exiting the third field, turn left and descend the hill, cross the bridge, then climb up the other side of the valley. At the top, you'll see the now very faded memorial stone at Carregwastad Point off to your right. Enjoy the beautiful views across the sea from this rarely visited spot, then retrace your steps back to Llandwnda.

98), and the cliff path is easy to find.

## Melin Tregwynt

MAP P.65
Near Castlemorris, SA62 5UX. 01348 891225, www.melintregwynt.co.uk. Mon–Fri 9.30am–5pm, Sat–Sun 10am–5pm. Free. Melin Tregwynt is a working woollen mill that's at least 200 years old, where visitors are welcome to explore and see the production process in action. The old water wheel, though no longer in use, can still be seen, among plenty of examples of more modern machinery. There are videos to help explain the mill's history, and some great information panels which give an overview of the history of fashion and Welsh cloth. Naturally, there's a shop on site at which you can purchase the mill's products (see page 66), and also a café which offers breakfasts, Sunday roasts, and an excellent beef cawl.

## Abermawr Beach

MAP P.65
A mostly shingle beach in a sheltered cove, you'll walk right along Abermawr if you're on the Pembrokeshire Coastal Path at the southwest point of Strumble Head. Abermawr holds a place in history as the eastern end of the first truly successful trans-Atlantic telegraph cable, though nowadays it's much more notable for being a great place to perfect your stone-skimming technique – there's an abundance of perfectly shaped flat pebbles on the shore. Just north of Abermawr is the smaller but equally attractive Aberbach beach.

## Abercastle

MAP P.65
The small village of Abercastle was once a centre of the local slate industry, but it's now a working fishing village and a good starting point for gorgeous rugged stretches of the coastal path, which afford great views out to sea and across to Strumble Head to the east. If you walk west from Abercastle, make sure to take the short diversion signposted from the cliff path to visit the very fine Neolithic burial chamber of Carreg Samson. This dolmen, consisting of a large capstone balanced above six supporting stones, is thought to be approximately 5,000 years old.

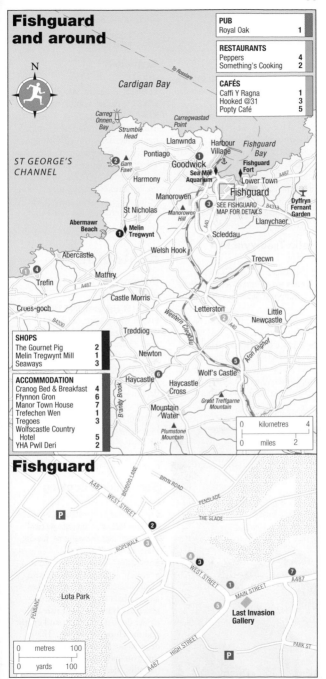

# Fishguard and around

| PUB | |
|---|---|
| Royal Oak | 1 |

| RESTAURANTS | |
|---|---|
| Peppers | 4 |
| Something's Cooking | 2 |

| CAFÉS | |
|---|---|
| Caffi Y Ragna | 1 |
| Hooked @31 | 3 |
| Popty Café | 5 |

| SHOPS | |
|---|---|
| The Gourmet Pig | 2 |
| Melin Tregwynt Mill | 1 |
| Seaways | 3 |

| ACCOMMODATION | |
|---|---|
| Cranog Bed & Breakfast | 4 |
| Ffynnon Gron | 6 |
| Manor Town House | 7 |
| Trefechen Wen | 1 |
| Tregoes | 3 |
| Wolfscastle Country Hotel | 5 |
| YHA Pwll Deri | 2 |

# Fishguard

# Shops

### The Gourmet Pig

MAP P.65

32 West St, Fishguard, SA65 9AD. 01348
874404, www.gourmetpig.co.uk. Mon–Sat
10am–4pm.

Fantastic deli selling a great range
of local produce, from Henry VII
cider through to Pembrokeshire
seaweed ketchup. It's an ideal spot
to stock up on picnic supplies if
you're planning a long day's walk
along the coast path, and it also
doubles up as an excellent coffee
shop if you're in need of a caffeine
boost.

### Melin Tregwynt Mill

MAP P.65

Near Castlemorris, SA62 5UX. 01348
891288, www.melintregwynt.co.uk. Mon–
Fri 9.30am–5pm, Sat–Sun 10am–5pm.

If you're after a Welsh wool product
– a coat, cushion, throw, purse,
slippers, you name it – this is a
great place to pick one up; there's
a huge selection in a variety of
styles and colours on sale in this
shop attached to the 200 year
old mill (see page 64). Other

Roast at Caffi y Ragna

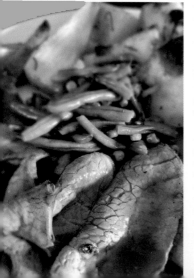

souvenirs – including love spoons,
chocolate, and local whisky – are
also available.

### Seaways

MAP P.65

12 West St, Fishguard, SA65 9AE. 01348
873433, www.seawaysbookshop.co.uk.
Mon–Sat 10am–5pm.

This small bookshop in Fishguard
has a great selection of both fiction
and non-fiction material, including
a very fine range of local interest
titles. If you want extra information
on Pembrokeshire's history, geology
or mythology – and much else
besides – chances are you'll find
it here.

# Restaurants

### Peppers

MAP P.65

16 West St, Fishguard, SA65 9AE. 01348
874540, www.peppers-hub.co.uk.
Mon–Sat 11am–8.30pm, Sun noon–3pm,
6pm–8.30pm.

One of Fishguard's most upmarket
restaurants, Peppers has a great
evening menu with an international
flavour – the Polish meatballs are
exceptionally good – as well as
offering lighter lunches. It also
hosts an art gallery, and there are
frequent jazz concerts here – check
the website for details on upcoming
events.

### Something's Cooking

MAP P.65

3 Haverfordwest Rd, Letterston, SA62 5SB.
01348 840621, www.sites.google.com/
view/somethingscooking/home. Tue–Sat
11am–2pm & 4.30pm–9pm.

Something's Cooking's menu is
generally seafood-focussed, with
options such as Solva crab cakes
and sea bass fillets, but its true
speciality is its excellent fish and
chips: the batter is light and crispy,
and the chips are perfect. The
desserts are fantastic too – make
sure you leave room for a slab of
banoffee pie.

The Royal Oak

# Cafés

### Caffi Y Ragna

MAP P.65

37 Ffordd Y Felin, Trefin, SA62 5AX. 01348 837204, www.facebook.com/caffiyragna. Tue–Sun 9am–4pm.

It's worth making a diversion from the cliff path into the attractive village of Trefin to stop at Caffi Y Ragna, which offers fabulous all-day breakfasts, hearty Sunday roasts, and great coffee. The carrot cake is a truly decadent treat. Behind the café is a small shop selling handicrafts, jewellery, and other souvenirs.

### Hooked @31

MAP P.65

31 West St, Fishguard, SA65 9AL. 01348 874657, www.hookedat31.co.uk. Wed–Sat noon–2pm & 4pm–8.30pm

An excellent fish and chip shop which offers daily specials, resulting in an ever-changing range of fabulous fish – but it's hard to beat the classic crispy battered cod and chips. There's also marvellous ice cream available – the Smarties Smash Up is perfect for those with an extremely sweet tooth. Takeaway only.

### Popty Café

MAP P.65

Market Square, Fishguard SA65 9HA. 07538 079473, www.facebook.com/Poptycafe. Daily 9am–3pm.

This small café on Fishguard's main square offers excellent coffee and great cakes, and has a very good reputation for its breakfasts. Service can be a little slow, but it's worth the wait.

# Pub

### Royal Oak

MAP P.65

Market Square, Fishguard, SA65 9HA. 01348 218632, www.royaloakfishguard.co.uk. Sun–Thu 11am–11pm, Fri–Sat 11am–midnight.

In 1797, the peace treaty between the English and the French was signed in the bar area of this friendly pub opposite Fishguard's town hall. While it's unlikely to be the site of any similarly important political events anytime soon, it's still a great place to enjoy a meal from the menu of usual pub favourites. If it's a warm day, consider eating on the beer terrace at the back, which affords decent views over the town and down to the sea.

# Newport and around

The principal settlement in Pembrokeshire's northeast corner is Newport, a pleasant arty town that's home to some lovely shops and excellent places to eat. It's overlooked by the Preseli Hills, a beautiful, stark area in which you'll find some great, if sometimes lonely, walking country peppered by much of the county's Neolithic heritage: burial chambers and stone circles are not uncommon here. Make sure to check out the region's medieval history at Cilgerran Castle and Nevern Church, while the coastal path around Ceibwr Bay showcases some of Pembrokeshire's finest geology amid spectacular cliff walking scenery.

## Newport

MAP P.70

Newport town centre, though short on sights, is an agreeable place to wander, with arty shops and welcoming cafés. The most obvious historic building, the castle, is now a private residence, but you can get a decent view of its exterior from Castle Street. Just to the castle's east is the 800-year-old St Mary's Church, which is of limited interest but does offer a small historical display about the church in its north transept.

## Kiln Odyn

MAP P.70

West St, Newport, SA42 0TF. 07805 141489, www.newportmemorialhall.co.uk/ medieval-kiln. 24h. Free.

Newport boasts the most intact surviving medieval pottery kiln in the UK. It can be seen as part of an engaging exhibition that's accessed down the side of the Memorial

Newport beach

Hall, which gives a thorough overview of the pottery-making process as well as a look at the wider society of medieval Newport.

## Newport Beach
MAP P.70

Newport's beach is a wide flat stretch of sand backed by grassy dunes, a couple of miles out of town to the north. It's overlooked by the towering mass of the large hill Carn Ingli, and is the last point of vehicular access to the eastbound coast path until Ceibwr Bay, some seven miles away. At the beach's east end, the Caffi Mawr is a convenient spot to grab an ice cream.

On your way to the beach from town, make a quick stop at the Neolithic burial chamber of Carreg Coetan, which is found in a small field near holiday cottages, signposted from the road. It's impressive to see how the lower stones continue to support the large, tilting boulder on top, some 5,000 years after it was erected (see box page 72).

## Carn Ingli
MAP P.70

If you fancy a good leg-stretcher with fine views as a reward, head up Church Street past St Mary's to begin the relatively easy two-hour ascent of Carn Ingli, so named because St Brynach reportedly lived here in quiet contemplation, accompanied only by angels (*ingli*). The hill was certainly once inhabited, whether by angels or not, as it's still possible to discern the stone embankments of an

Iron Age hill fort and nearby Bronze Age hut circles.

## Church of St Brynach
MAP P.70
Nevern, Newport, SA42 0NF. www.nevern-church.org.uk. No set hours; likely to be daily 9am–7pm. Free.

Two miles east of Newport is the small village of Nevern, where you'll find a couple of interesting historical sites. The church of St Brynach, set in an atmospheric churchyard filled with yew trees, was first founded in the sixth century, but it's thought that the oldest part of the current structure dates from around 1380. In the churchyard you'll find several curiosities, foremost among them the 'bleeding yew', which secretes a blood-coloured sap. It's the second yew on the right as you enter the churchyard. St Brynach's is also home to a beautiful Celtic cross, as well as the Vitalianus and Magnoconus Stones, both of which bear inscriptions in both Latin and the ancient Irish Ogham tongue.

## Nevern Castle
MAP P.70
Nevern, Newport, SA42 0NF. www.neverncastle.wales. 24h. Free.

Little remains of Nevern Castle other than the earthworks and the distinctive motte, but even so, it's still an evocative site with engaging information boards dotted around to help bring the history of the place to life. The castle lasted less than a century; it was built in 1108

## Medieval stone crosses

Early Christians in Pembrokeshire working in the centuries after the Roman departure in 410 AD, produced a huge number of carvings in stone, many of which can still be seen in churchyards across the county. The Ogham language stones at St Brynach's church in Nevern make a great place to start, but other fine examples can be found in St David's church in Bridell and St Brynach's church in Pontfaen. The tall Celtic cross monuments were later works, dating from the tenth or eleventh century, and the examples at Nevern and Carew are among the finest in Wales.

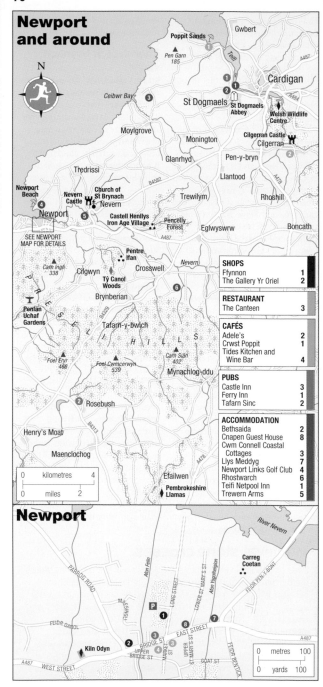

# Newport and around

Gwbert

Poppit Sands

Pen Garn
185

Teifi

Cardigan

Ceibwr Bay

St Dogmaels

St Dogmaels Abbey

Welsh Wildlife Centre

Moylgrove

Monington

Cilgerran Castle
Cilgerran

Glanrhyd

Pen-y-bryn

Tredrissi

Trewilym

Llantood

Rhoshill

Newport Beach

Nevern Castle
Nevern

Church of St Brynach

Boncath

Newport

Castell Henllys Iron Age Village

Pencelly Forest

Eglwyswrw

SEE NEWPORT MAP FOR DETAILS

Carn Ingli
338

Pentre Ifan

Cilgwyn

Crosswell

Nevern

Penlan Uchaf Gardens

Tŷ Canol Woods

Brynberian

P R E S E L I   H I L L S

Tafarn-y-bwlch

Foel Eryr
468

Foel Cwmcerwyn
539

Carn Siân
402

Mynachlog-ddu

Rosebush

Henry's Moat

Maenclochog

Efailwen

Pembrokeshire Llamas

| 0 | kilometres | | 4 |
| 0 | miles | 2 | |

## SHOPS
| Ffynnon | 1 |
| The Gallery Yr Oriel | 2 |

## RESTAURANT
| The Canteen | 3 |

## CAFÉS
| Adele's | 2 |
| Crwst Poppit | 1 |
| Tides Kitchen and Wine Bar | 4 |

## PUBS
| Castle Inn | 3 |
| Ferry Inn | 1 |
| Tafarn Sinc | 2 |

## ACCOMMODATION
| Bethsaida | 2 |
| Cnapen Guest House | 8 |
| Cwm Connell Coastal Cottages | 3 |
| Llys Meddyg | 7 |
| Newport Links Golf Club | 4 |
| Rhostwarch | 6 |
| Teifi Netpool Inn | 1 |
| Trewern Arms | 5 |

# Newport

River Nevern

PARROG ROAD

Afon Felin

LONG STREET

LOWER ST MARY'S ST

Afon Ysgolheigion

Carreg Coetan

FEIDR PEN-Y-BONT

MILLSTONE LANE

FEIDR GANOL

EAST STREET

BRIDGE ST

UPPER BRIDGE ST

MARKET ST

UPPER ST MARY'S ST

GOAT ST

FEIDR BENTICK

A487

WEST STREET

Kiln Odyn

| 0 | metres | 100 |
| 0 | yards | 100 |

and destroyed in 1195, probably to prevent it falling into the hands of the encroaching Anglo-Normans. The castle's most notable inhabitant was the ambitious and wily Prince of Deheubarth, Rhys ap Gruffydd, who enjoyed a spell as a prisoner of his own sons here in the 1190s.

## Ty Canol Woods

MAP P.70

Well-marked trails lead you through the tangled and mossy forest of Ty Canol to the craggy summit of Meibbeg Owen. The woods, which are an ideal habitat for many species of lichen, are ancient and mysterious – the sort of place you could almost imagine bumping into a wise old wizard – and the view from the summit is wide-ranging and beautiful.

## Castell Henllys Iron Age Village

MAP P.70

Meline, near Crymych, SA41 3UR. 01239 891319, www.pembrokeshirecoast.wales/ castell-henllys. Daily Apr–Oct 10am–5pm, Nov–Mar 10am–4pm. £5.50.

Castell Henllys – literally "the castle of the old court" – was a site of some considerable importance during the Iron Age. A hill fort constructed in an easily defensible position, it was inhabited for some 400 years until around 50 BC, when it was abandoned for reasons unknown. Today, reconstructed Iron Age huts stand on the hilltop, replete with internal decorations and furnishings. The fort's enthusiastic and knowledgeable staff are always happy to discuss the history and function of this fascinating site. Don't forget to say hello to the pigs – they're a cross between the Tamworth breed and a wild boar. The visitor centre sports a café and a small shop.

## Ceibwr Bay

MAP P.70

The small and shingly Ceibwr Bay is one of the best places around the coast to see Pembrokeshire's remarkable geology. To get the best view, take the short path to the small headland on the west side – look east to see the spectacular folded cliffs on the other side of the bay, west for a fine view of a pair of jagged stacks in the sea, and straight ahead to see the waves crashing over rocky shelves that lie submerged in the water. If you fancy a longer walk, the coastal path in either direction here affords stunning and rugged scenery.

## Poppit Sands

MAP P.70

Poppit Sands is a large sandy beach backed by grassy dunes, with great waves for bodyboarding. This is the northern start/end point of the Pembrokeshire Coast Path, and the section from here is a long and remote stretch, with no further vehicular access until Ceibwr Bay.

## St Dogmaels Abbey

MAP P.70

Shingrig, St Dogmaels, SA43 3DX. 01239 615389, www.stdogmaelsabbey.org. uk. Abbey 24h; visitor centre Mon–Sat 9.30am–3.30pm. Free.

St Dogmaels Abbey

The ruins of the small St Dogmaels Abbey are worth exploring; established in 1115, it is thought to stand on the site of an older monastery that had been established by St Dogmael himself in the sixth century. The adjacent St Thomas Church is home to the Sagranus Stone, which – like similar stones at Nevern's St Brynach (see page 69) – acts as a sort of Rosetta Stone that enabled the translation of the Ogham alphabet which was used in early medieval Ireland.

## Welsh Wildlife Centre

MAP P.70

Cilgerran, SA43 2TB. 01239 621600, www. welshwildlife.org/visitor-centres/the-welsh-wildlife-centre. Wed–Sun 10am–4pm. Free; parking charges apply (£4 daily).
The Welsh Wildlife Centre offers a great opportunity to see a variety of local wildlife, including herons, kingfishers, and – if you're lucky – otters. Paved paths and boardwalks lead you around the centre's woodland and marshes, with periodic hides and engaging info boards. For the more adventurous, the centre also runs canoe and kayaking trips down the Teifi Gorge (£35 per adult). The modern visitor centre boasts a café, toilets, and a shop selling outdoor wear, souvenirs, and an excellent range of local interest books, particularly focussing on wildlife.

If you're planning to visit often, it may be worth considering investing in a membership, which will entitle you to free parking and free entry to Dinefwr Park in Llandeilo (see page 85).

## Cilgerran Castle

MAP P.70

Cilgerran, SA43 2SF. 01239 621339, www. nationaltrust.org.uk/cilgerran-castle. Daily 10am–4pm. Free.
Cilgerran Castle, situated in a strategic spot above the River Teifi,

# Pembrokeshire's Neolithic heritage

There are reminders of Pembrokeshire's Neolithic past to be found throughout the county, but this northeast corner is the best place to get on the trail of our prehistoric ancestors. Ancient hill forts can be found throughout this region, including at Foel Drygarn and at Garn Fawr on Strumble Head, and you'll also find a stone circle at Gors Fawr. Perhaps the most impressive memorials to Pembrokeshire's ancient peoples are the burial chambers which still litter the landscape. One of the most perfect is found at Pentre Ifan, which is easily accessible from the A487, and other excellent examples include Carreg Coetan, a mere five minutes' walk from Newport's centre, and the harder-to-find Gwal y Filiast, which is set in atmospheric woodland a little south of the village of Llanglydwen.

Intriguingly, geological research in 2021 uncovered evidence that the stones used for the construction of Stonehenge – some 170 miles to the southeast – were quarried and may originally have stood here in Pembrokeshire, in a stone circle at Waun Mawn in the Preseli Hills, before being transported to their current position. This is all the more fascinating given a medieval legend, put about by the notoriously imaginative Geoffrey of Monmouth, that claims Stonehenge was moved from its original location to Wiltshire – though in Geoffrey's version it was brought from Ireland by the wizard Merlin. Geoffrey's account has been discredited for centuries, but it seems there may be a grain of truth to it after all.

# A walk at Rosebush

The now disused slate quarry just outside Rosebush village (map page 70) is a beautiful place for a short 45-minute walk. Turn left out of the Tafarn Sinc pub (see page 75) and head along the bridleway past a row of cottages. As you reach a couple of ruined mining buildings, take the path that goes uphill on the right – at the top here is an old mine shaft that plunges deep into the hill.

Return to the ruined buildings and then take the next track running diagonally upwards on the right. It emerges at a small triangle of paths – take the right-hand one and pass between two great stone outcrops to find a stunning turquoise pool. It's an absolutely magical spot.

Retrace your steps to the triangle and take the other path, which winds along the edge of the quarry amid piles of slate and past a deep blasted pit, now half-filled with water – keep an eye on the kids here, and dogs are best kept on the lead. Eventually the path passes out of the quarry and bends left at a fence. Turn left again at the bottom and follow the bridleway back to Rosebush, or if you fancy a longer exploration, paths lead off to the right into Pantmaenog Forest.

was built in about 1100, but its current form is largely due to the thirteenth century rebuilding works of William Marshal the Younger, son and namesake of the famous Earl of Pembroke (see page 41). You can climb both the east and west towers for views over the castle and surrounding valley.

## Pembrokeshire Llamas

MAP P.70

Glanrhydwilym, Rhydwilym, Llandissilio, SA66 7QH. 07539 892519, www.llamas. wales. By appointment. £45.

Operating out of Glanrhydwilym Farm, a herd of ten llamas are available to stroll with you through the wooded countryside on the Black Cleddau river valley. The llamas made international news in May 2020 when they began delivering food to residents of the valley, thereby saving them the risk of exposure to Covid-19 in supermarkets! The llamas' lives are a little quieter now, but they're still very keen to walk with visitors.

## Penlan-Uchaf Gardens

MAP P.70

Gwaun Valley, Fishguard, SA65 9UA. 01348 881388, www.visitpembrokeshire.com/ attraction-listing/penlan-uchaf-gardens. Daily 10am–dusk. £3.

Well tucked away, Penlan Uchaf is a set of hillside gardens cut through by a stream with wonderful views over the valley. They contain thousands of miniature flowering and alpine plants, and acres of herbs and wildflowers together with some impressive dwarf conifers.

Pembrokeshire Llamas

# Shops

## Ffynnon

MAP P.70

Long St, Newport, SA42 0TJ. 01239 821112,
www.facebook.com/ffynnonhomestore.
Mon & Wed–Sat 10am–5pm.

This lovely little vintage shop sells a
variety of upmarket gifts and items
for the home – it's a good place
to pick up attractive kitchenware,
a Melin Tregywnt throw, or some
local chocolate, among many
other options. A perfect spot for
browsing their wide collection of
gorgeously-designed coffee table
books.

## The Gallery Yr Oriel

MAP P.70

5 Bridge St, Newport, SA42 0TB. 01239
821514, www.thegallery-yroriel.com.
Mon–Sat 10am–5pm.

A small and sweet gallery selling
sculptures, jewellery and artwork,
much of it with a local flavour and
by local artists. There's a great range
of styles on show here, and though
the artwork themselves aren't cheap,
casual browsers are welcome – it's
almost as much a gallery as a shop!

Pizza at The Canteen

# Restaurant

## The Canteen

MAP P.70

Dolphin House, Market St, Newport,
SA42 0PH. 01239 820131, www.
thecanteennewport.com. Tue–Sat
10am–2pm & 6pm–8.30pm.

This small and friendly restaurant
serves excellent pizzas with a great
selection of toppings, including
some tasty vegetarian options, and
a good range of local Bluestone ales
to wash them down with. There's
attractive artwork available to buy
on the walls.

# Cafés

## Adele's

MAP P.70

High St, Cilgerran, SA43 2SQ. 07495
614651, www.facebook.com/
adelescafeCilgerran. Tue–Fri 10am–3pm,
Sat 10am–2pm.

Perfectly situated for a refuelling
stop after visiting Cilgerran
Castle, Adele's is a great place for
a coffee and homemade cake. The
tiffin is a good option, but the
cheesecakes are truly magnificent.
They regularly come in strawberry,
lemon, and mixed berry flavours,
though there is a rotation of other
special flavours too – if you're
lucky, you might visit on an Eton
Mess cheesecake day! Light and
main meals are also available.

## Crwst Poppit

MAP P.70

Poppit, St Dogmaels SA43 3LN. 01239
920186, www.crwst.cymru/crwst-poppit-
sands. Tue–Sun 10am–4pm.

This little hut just off Poppit Sands
is a godsend if you're wanting a
tasty lunch or a cup of coffee to
enjoy on the beach. There's also
locally-made ice cream for those
in search of a sweet treat, and they
even sell ice cream that's suitable for
your canine friends – so nobody has
to miss out!

The Castle Inn

### Tides Kitchen and Wine Bar

MAP P.70

Market St, Newport, SA42 0PH. 01239 820777, www.business.facebook.com/ marketstreetnewport. Wed 9am–3pm, Thu–Fri 9am–3pm & 6pm–11pm, Sat 9am–3pm & 6pm–10pm.

Sit at the outside tables at Tides for a great view up the street to the castle. It's an agreeable place that offers light deli lunches – including an excellent local crab tart – as well as coffee and cakes in the daytime, plus larger meals and a fine selection of wines in the evening.

## Pubs

### Castle Inn

MAP P.70

Bridge St, Newport, SA42 0TB. 01239 820742, www.castleinnpembs.co.uk. Wed–Sat noon–2pm & 5.30pm–8pm, Sun noon–2pm.

A very friendly pub on Newport's main street that serves upmarket pub meals. The lamb and leek sausages, accompanied by parsley mashed potatoes, are an excellent choice. The Castle also has a few

rooms and is a pleasant place for an overnight stay.

### Ferry Inn

MAP P.70

Poppit Road, St Dogmaels, SA43 3LF. 01239 615172, www.theferryinn.co.uk. Wed 5.30pm–8.30pm, Thu–Sat noon–2.30pm & 5.30pm–8.30pm, Sun noon–3pm.

This large and welcoming gastropub on the banks of the River Teifi has a great outdoor terrace and a fantastic menu – try to be there on Sunday for an excellent roast dinner. The desserts are rather fine too, if you have room.

### Tafarn Sinc

MAP P.70

Bryn Ter, Rosebush, SA66 7QU. 01437 532214, www.tafarnsinc.cymru/eng/index. php. Daily noon–10pm.

This marvellous community-owned pub is housed at the site of the former Rosebush Station; outside, there's a very small section of the railway track remaining and a great mock-up of passengers waiting for the train in homage to the pub's history. The menu is excellent Welsh fare, and the beer garden has lovely views over the Preselis.

# Further afield

There's plenty to keep you entertained in Pembrokeshire, but it's also worth stepping beyond its borders once or twice during your stay; the surrounding regions have a great deal to offer. In the north, it's easy to hop across the county border into Ceredigion to enjoy a trip to Cardigan and experience the fantastic beaches and boat trips in Cardigan Bay. Down south, meanwhile, there are plenty of reasons to head out of Pembrokeshire to visit the many beautiful castles in the region, particularly Carreg Cennan, and it's also here that you'll find the marvellous National Botanic Garden of Wales. Those of a literary bent may enjoy a trip to Laugharne to visit the home of Dylan Thomas, one of Wales' most highly regarded poets.

## Around Cardigan

Just across the border from Pembrokeshire on the north coast, Cardigan is an attractive and bustling little town with an interesting castle, great shopping, and excellent food. It's a nice place to base yourself to enjoy the beaches along Cardigan Bay and wildlife-spotting boat trips, or to head further inland to check out the quirky National Wool Museum and visit the pretty Cenarth Falls.

## Cardigan
MAP P.78

The pretty town of Cardigan on the banks of the River Teifi was once one of Wales' most important ports, with a particular speciality

Aberporth

# Eisteddfod

While exploring Cardigan Castle, you shouldn't miss the section on the Eisteddfod, the Welsh national music festival, in which musicians and performing artists compete to win the title of Bard. The first recorded example of an eisteddfod was held by Lord Rhys ap Gruffordd in 1176, in celebration of the completion of Cardigan Castle's construction, and these competitions have been held regularly ever since, though they suffered a decline during the sixteenth and seventeenth centuries. Today, the most important event on the Eisteddfod calendar is the annual National Eisteddfod, which usually takes place in August and is held in a different location each year.

in exporting Welsh wool to France for the production of tapestries, but trade declined when the mouth of the Teifi silted up in the nineteenth century. These days there's little evidence of its former status, but it is a sprightly little town, and an attractive place to browse the independent shops and cafés. The picturesque High Street leads up to the spiky turrets of the Guildhall and the bustling covered market, an eclectic mix of locally produced food and browsable oddities. Leading off the High Street, narrow thoroughfares come crammed with Georgian and Victorian buildings.

## Cardigan Castle

MAP P.78
Green St, Cardigan, SA43 1JA. 01239 615131, www.cardigancastle.com. Daily Apr–Oct 10am–4pm, Nov–Mar Tue–Sat 10am–4pm. £6.
Little remains of the medieval Cardigan Castle, built by Lord Rhys ap Gruffordd in the 1170s, as it suffered considerable damage during the Civil War in 1644. One tower is built into the walls of a Georgian manor house that now occupies the site, which is packed full of a medley of fantastic exhibitions about the history of Cardigan and its castle, including a fascinating set on the castle's last private owner, Barbara Wood, who only moved out in 1999. Interactive exhibits make the place really interesting

for kids. Elsewhere on the castle grounds you'll find a kitchen garden, a very proud wood sculpture of Lord Rhys, and a whalebone arch. The surviving ramparts offer decent if not stunning views over the Teifi.

## Aberporth and Tresaith

MAP P.78
Five miles or so northeast of Cardigan you'll find the small villages of Aberporth and Tresaith, both of which are blessed with gorgeous beaches of golden sands. Tresaith has the added bonus of a fairly large waterfall cascading from the cliffs into the sea – head to the northeast end of the beach to see it.

## Cenarth Falls

MAP P.78
A fine set of waterfalls on the Teifi river, Cenarth Falls are beautiful the whole year round, but it's particularly worth stopping by in autumn for a chance to see salmon leaping the falls as they return to their spawning grounds. Park in the car park on the north side of the Cenarth bridge and follow the boardwalk path to the left-hand side of the river, which affords fine views of the falls and the abandoned mill and water wheel on the opposite bank. Cenarth is famous for its coracles – for a good history of this ancient type of boat, check out the National Coracle Centre (01239 710980,

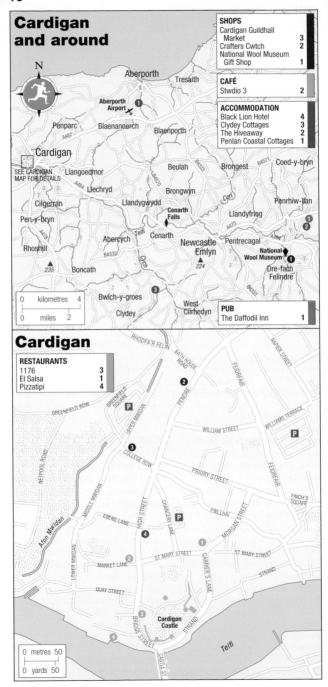

# Cardigan and around

N

Aberporth
Tresaith
Aberporth Airport ①
Penparc
Blaenannerch
Blaenporth
Cardigan
SEE CARDIGAN MAP FOR DETAILS
Llangoedmor
Beulah
Brongest
Coed-y-bryn
Llechryd
Brongwyn
Cilgerran
Llandygwydd
Cenarth Falls
Llandyfriog
Penrhiw-llan
Pen-y-bryn
Abercych
Cenarth
Newcastle Emlyn
Pentrecagal
② ①
Rhoshill
235
Boncath
Bwlch-y-groes ③
Teifi
Dyfi
224
National Wool Museum ①
Dre-fach Felindre

A487 A484 B4570 B4571 B4333 Ceri A475 A484 B4333 A478 B4332 B4335

0 kilometres 4
0 miles 2

West Cilrhedyn
Clydey

**SHOPS**
Cardigan Guildhall Market — 3
Crafters Cwtch — 2
National Wool Museum Gift Shop — 1

**CAFÉ**
Stwdio 3 — 2

**ACCOMMODATION**
Black Lion Hotel — 4
Clydey Cottages — 3
The Hiveaway — 2
Penlan Coastal Cottages — 1

**PUB**
The Daffodil Inn — 1

# Cardigan

**RESTAURANTS**
1176 — 3
El Salsa — 1
Pizzatipi — 4

RHODFA'R FELIN
BATH HOUSE ROAD
NAPIER STREET
FENDRE
FELDRFAIR
WILLIAMS TERRACE
GREENFIELD SQUARE
GREENFIELD ROW
UPPER MWLDAN
WILLIAM STREET
②
COLLEGE ROW ③
PRIORY STREET
NETPOOL ROAD
MIDDLE MWLDAN
PWLLHAI
FINCH'S SQUARE
EBENS LANE
HIGH STREET
CHANCERY LANE
④
Afon Mwldan
LOWER MWLDAN
MARKET LANE ②
ST MARY STREET
①
ST MARY STREET
CARRIER'S LANE
MORGAN STREET
STRAND
QUAY STREET
③
Cardigan Castle
BRIDGE STREET
CASTLE ST
STRAND
Teifi
④
FELDRFAIR

0 metres 50
0 yards 50

# Cardigan Bay wildlife

Cardigan Bay stretches all the way from Strumble Head near Fishguard round to Bardsey Island off the coast of Gwynedd, making it the largest bay in Wales. It's no surprise, then, that it's home to a huge variety of marine life, particularly bottlenose dolphins, grey seals and harbour porpoise, as well as less frequently sighted creatures such as basking sharks and minke whales. If you want to get out on the water to catch a glimpse of some of this abundant wildlife, there are numerous operators all along the Bay who run boat trips in summer – closest to Cardigan, consider the excellent A Bay to Remember (Patch beach, Gwbert, Cardigan SA43 1PP, 01239 623558, www. baytoremember.co.uk).

open by appointment only) while you're here. There are some quant souvenir shops selling local chutneys, jams and the like, as well as several lovely pubs and cafés to detain you, all within 5 minutes' walking distance of the falls.

## National Wool Museum

MAP P.78
Dre-fach Felindre, near Newcastle Emlyn, SA44 5UP. 0300 1112333, www.museum. wales/wool. Tue–Sat 10am–5pm. Free.
Housed in a large former mill, the National Wool Museum displays equipment and demonstrates the use of the machinery, alongside engaging information boards detailing the history of wool production, often in the form of reproduction newspaper headlines telling the story of events at the mill. The museum is punctuated by occasionally interactive exhibits and fascinating facts – you'll discover the origin of the phrase "to be on tenterhooks", find out how many miles of cloth one worker could produce in a week, and learn the difference between a quilt and a blanket. Upstairs, there's a small exhibition of historical woollen fashions – the 1960s outfits are fantastic.

## Around St Clears

Travellers tend to whizz through St Clears on their way down to Pembrokeshire, and while there's not a whole lot to detain you in

St Clears itself, it is worth making a detour off the A40 to explore the surrounding region. Rich in medieval history and the literary heritage of Dylan Thomas, you'll also find attractive countryside and the enormous stretch of Pendine Sands, which are an easy hop from the southeast corner of Pembrokeshire.

## Pendine Sands

MAP P.80
The wide expanse of Pendine Sands earned its place in history as the site of various land speed records that were set here between 1924 and 1927 by Malcolm Campbell and J. G. Parry-Thomas. Campbell set an initial record of 146 mph in aero-engineered car called a Sunbeam 350HP, and subsequently became the first person to reach 150 mph, after which Parry-Thomas made it to 171 mph and Campbell then upped the record to 174 mph. Parry-Thomas attempted to exceed this, but tragedy struck; he was killed when his car crashed. It's rather quieter at Pendine these days, but it is a lovely place for a day out at the beach. A museum and visitor centre have been under construction for some years, and had no expected date of opening at time of writing, but when complete it will tell the compelling story of the race to set ever-faster speed records.

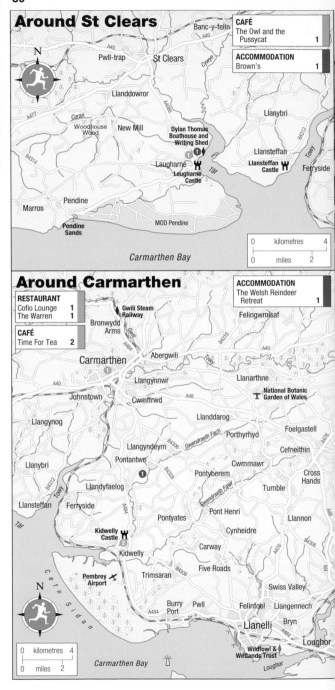

# Around St Clears

Banc-y-felin

Pwll-trap
St Clears

Llanddowror

Coran
Woodhouse Wood
New Mill

Llanybri

**Dylan Thomas Boathouse and Writing Shed**

Laugharne
**Laugharne Castle**

Llansteffan
**Llansteffan Castle**

Ferryside

Marros
Pendine

**Pendine Sands**

MOD Pendine

*Carmarthen Bay*

| CAFÉ | |
|---|---|
| The Owl and the Pussycat | 1 |

| ACCOMMODATION | |
|---|---|
| Brown's | 1 |

| 0 | kilometres | 4 |
| 0 | miles | 2 |

# Around Carmarthen

| RESTAURANT | |
|---|---|
| Cofio Lounge | 1 |
| The Warren | 1 |

| CAFÉ | |
|---|---|
| Time For Tea | 2 |

| ACCOMMODATION | |
|---|---|
| The Welsh Reindeer Retreat | 1 |

**Gwili Steam Railway**

Bronwydd Arms

Felingwmisaf

Carmarthen

Abergwili

Llanarthne

Llangynnwr

**National Botanic Garden of Wales**

Johnstown

Cwmffrwd

Llanddarog

Llangynog

Porthyrhyd

Foelgastell

Gwendraeth Fach

Llangyndeyrn

Cwmmawr

Cefneithin

Pontantwn

Pontyberem

Cross Hands

Llanybri

Llandyfaelog

Gwendraeth Fawr

Tumble

Ferryside

Pontyates

Pont Henri

Llannon

Llansteffan

**Kidwelly Castle**

Cynheidre

Kidwelly

Carway

**Pembrey Airport**

Trimsaran

Five Roads

Swiss Valley

Burry Port

Pwll

Felinfoel

Llangennech

Llanelli

Bryn

Loughor

**Wildfowl & Wetlands Trust**

Loughor

*Cefn Sidan*

*Carmarthen Bay*

| 0 | kilometres | 4 |
| 0 | miles | 2 |

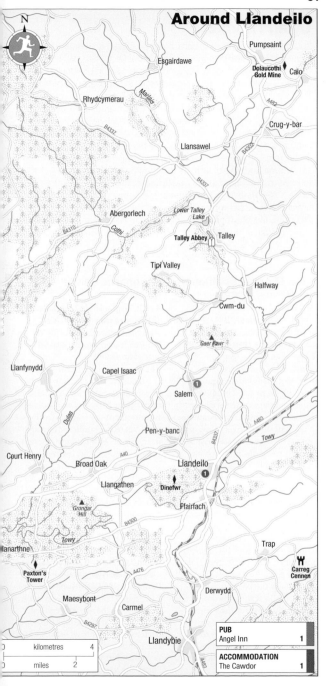

# Around Llandeilo

N

Pumpsaint

Esgairdawe

Dolaucothi
Gold Mine

Caio

Rhydcymerau

Marlas

A482

Crug-y-bar

B4337

Llansawel

B4302

B4337

Abergorlech

Lower Talley
Lake

Cothi

Talley Abbey

Talley

B4310

Tipi Valley

Halfway

Cwm-du

Gaer Fawr

Llanfynydd

Capel Isaac

Salem

1

A483

Towy

Pen-y-banc

B4337

Dulas

Court Henry

A40

Broad Oak

Llandeilo

1

Llangathen

Dinefwr

Grongar
Hill

Ffairfach

B4300

Towy

Trap

Llanarthne

A476

Carreg
Cennen

Paxton's
Tower

Derwydd

Maesybont

Carmel

B4297

Llandybie

A483

| PUB | |
|---|---|
| Angel Inn | 1 |

| ACCOMMODATION | |
|---|---|
| The Cawdor | 1 |

kilometres 4

miles 2

# Dylan Thomas

Dylan Thomas (1914–53), born into a comfortably middle-class family in Swansea, was the quintessential Celt – fiery, verbose, richly talented and habitually drunk. He arrived in London as a broke 20-year-old in 1934, weeks before the appearance of his first volumes of poetry, and after marrying his wife Caitlin in 1937 returned to Wales, settling in Laugharne. Despite his evident hedonism – he spent many days boozing in Brown's Hotel – Thomas was a disciplined writer, honing some of the twentieth century's most instantly recognizable poetry, including *Do Not Go Gentle Into That Good Night* and the beautiful *Fern Hill*. His death in 1953 came just one month after he had put the finishing touches to what many regard as his masterpiece, the "play for voices", *Under Milk Wood*. Describing the dreams, thoughts and lives of a Welsh seaside community called Llareggub over the course of 24 hours, the play has never dipped out of fashion and has lured some of Wales' greatest stars, including Richard Burton, Anthony Hopkins and Michael Sheen, to the role of the narrator.

## Dylan Thomas Boathouse and Writing Shed

MAP P.80
Dylan's Walk, Laugharne, SA33 4SD. 01994 427420, www.dylanthomasboathouse. com. Daily Apr–Sep 10am–5pm, Oct–Mar 10.30am–3pm. £4.75.

In the 1930s, Laugharne was home to a man widely regarded as one of the finest Welsh poets of the twentieth century, Dylan Thomas, who found the boathouse on the harbour front a happy and conducive place to work. Visitors can view the parlour, which has been restored to the appearance it's likely to have had when Dylan and his wife Caitlin lived here in 1938. Upstairs, there's an engaging film as well as numerous artefacts and photographs of Dylan's career. A large model of Llareggub, the fictional village from his famous radio play *Under Milk Wood*, takes pride of place.

Just down the path from the boathouse back towards the village centre is the writing shed where Dylan worked in the later years of his life. You may also wish to visit Dylan's grave, in the churchyard of St Martin's at the north end of the village.

## Laugharne Castle

MAP P.80
King St, Laugharne, SA33 4FA. 03000 252239, www.cadw.gov.wales/visit/places-to-visit/laugharne-castle. Apr–Jul Thu–Mon 10am–5pm, daily Aug–Oct 10am–5pm. £4.20.

The imposing Laugharne Castle is a medieval construction, with Elizabethan expansions undertaken by Sir John Perrot, who also made improvements to Carew Castle (see page 52). After suffering damage in the Civil War, the castle became the picturesque ruin beloved by many visitors over the years, including Dylan Thomas. There's a pleasant seafront path from the castle car park to Dylan Thomas's boathouse.

## Llansteffan Castle

MAP P.80
Church Road, Llansteffan, SA33 5LW. www. cadw.gov.wales/visit/places-to-visit/llansteffan-castle. Daily 10am–4pm. Free.

Llansteffan Castle stands on a hill overlooking the attractive village of Llansteffan; it's thought to have been a fortified site as far back as the Iron Age. Much of the castle is ruined, but it's still possible to climb the towers for fantastic views

Laugharne Castle

over the castle itself and the nearby beach.

## Around Carmarthen

If you're approaching Pembrokeshire along the most obvious route, the A48, you'll be bypassing Carmarthen on your way. If you have the time and the inclindation, consider making a few stops en route in this region: the National Botanic Garden of Wales is an absolute must, and nature enthusiasts will enjoy the excellent Wildfowl and Wetlands Trust in Llanelli.

## Carmarthen

MAP P.80

The county town of Carmarthenshire, Carmarthen nowadays is not a hugely exciting place, but it does have considerable history and mythology to it – medieval writers claimed it to be the birthplace of the wizard Merlin, and his alleged resting place, Bryn Myrddin, is just outside the town. Perhaps the most obvious attraction in Carmarthen is the remains of the Norman castle, whose keep you can climb for a view over the town

and is a great place for a picnic on a sunny day.

## Gwili Steam Railway

MAP P.80

Bronwydd Arms, SA33 6HT. 01267 238213, www.gwili-railway.co.uk. Daily; departures at 10.30am, 1pm and 3.30pm. £13.

Steam train enthusiasts will have a field day at this fantastic railway that runs through a beautiful landscape. Originally part of the Carmarthen to Aberystwyth line that was closed in 1965, the track stations and locomotives have been lovingly restored by enthusiastic volunteers, allowing you to relive the golden age of railways. On special occasions you'll be able to enjoy themed train rides, including Halloween ghost trains and murder mystery evenings.

## National Botanic Garden of Wales

MAP P.80

Llanarthne, SA32 8HN. 01558 667149, www.botanicgarden.wales. Daily Apr–Oct 10am–6pm, Nov–Mar 10am–4pm. £13.75.

The National Botanic Garden of Wales could easily detain you for a full day, such is its size and beauty

– and what a lovely day it would be! You should make sure not to miss the gorgeous walled garden and the attached Tropical House, but perhaps pride of place goes to the Great Glasshouse, an elegant building that is known for being the world's largest single-span glasshouse. Elsewhere, there are pretty lakes, peaceful woodland walks, and limitless gorgeous plant and flower displays, as well as the opportunity to enjoy displays from the British Bird of Prey Centre. If you need a rest stop after all that, the Caffi Botanica offers a great range of delicious food and drink, and there's also a very fine garden shop on site.

## Kidwelly Castle

MAP P.80
Castle Road, Kidwelly, SA17 5BQ. 03000 252239, www.cadw.gov.wales/visit/places-to-visit/kidwelly-castle. Daily Mar–Jun 10am–5pm, Jul–Aug 10am–6pm, Sep–Oct 9.30am–5pm, Nov–Feb 10am–4pm. £5.80.
A fine example of a thirteenth-century fortress, it's great fun exploring the passages and towers of Kidwelly Castle. The ground floor of the gatehouse is home to

The Glasshouse at the Botanic Garden

an interesting historical display, and you'll enjoy fine views over the castle from the top of the southwest tower. At the edge of the car park, there's a memorial to the medieval Princess Gwenllian, one-time inhabitant of this castle, who led a doomed attack on an Anglo-Norman army in 1136 and is considered a great Welsh heroine.

## Wildfowl & Wetlands Trust

MAP P.80
Llwynhendy, Llanelli, SA14 9SH. www.wwt.org.uk/wetland-centres/llanelli. Daily 9.30am–5pm. £10.10.
An extensive network of paths lead around the pools and hides of the Wildfowl & Wetlands Trust Centre at Llanelli, set in the marshy lands by the Loughor Estuary. Bird enthusiasts will be in their element – there's a huge variety of different species to see, including a flock of flamingos, whose bright pink feathers stand out dramatically against the sometimes bleak landscape. In the summer, canoe safaris (£9) are available to explore otherwise inaccessible sections of the wetlands.

# Rhys ap Gruffordd

If you've been visiting the castles of Pembrokeshire, Ceredigion and Carmarthenshire, you're very likely to have come across the name Rhys ap Gruffordd. This twelfth-century Prince of Deheubarth – a swathe of territory incorporating much of southwest Wales – spent many years engaged in warfare against the English kings Henry II and Richard the Lionheart, as well as against other Welsh rulers and even, in later life, his own sons. This military career resulted in a need for castles, and consequently he constructed or rebuilt many fortresses in this part of the country; among others, Dinefwr, Carreg Cennan, Nevern and Cardigan are Rhys' work. He died in 1197 and is buried at St Davids Cathedral.

## Around Llandeilo

Llandeilo is a small town just west of the Brecon Beacons National Park, with several interesting attractions within easy reach. The National Trust sites of Dinefwr and Dolaucothi Gold Mine are both fascinating spots with long histories, and the isolated Carreg Cennan is easily one of the most beautiful castles that Wales has to offer.

## Dinefwr

MAP P.81

Dinefwr Park, Newton House, Llandeilo, SA19 6RT. 01558 825910, www. nationaltrust.org.uk/dinefwr. Grounds daily Apr–Oct 10am–5pm, Nov–Mar 10am–4pm; Newton House daily Apr–Oct 10.30am–4.30pm, Nov–Mar Sat–Sun 10.30am–3.30pm. Free entry to grounds; entry to house £8; parking charges apply (£5 daily).

The National Trust estate of Dinefwr consists of Newton House, which looks like the sort of place Batman might live, as well as a medieval castle and substantial walking trails around the deer park. Newton House was built in the late seventeenth century, though its current magnificently gothic form dates back to the 1850s when it was altered to bring it into line with Victorian architectural trends. The medieval castle was fortified by Rhys ap Gruffordd, the apparently tireless prince of Deheubarth.

## Paxton's Tower

MAP P.81

Near Llanarthney, SA32 8HX. www. nationaltrust.org.uk/features/feel-on-top-of-the-world-at-paxtons-tower-. Daily 8am–6pm. Free.

The National Trust site of Paxton's Tower consists of a nineteenth-century folly atop a hill; climb up to it for views of the surrounding countryside. Built by Sir William Paxton, ostensibly to honour Nelson's naval victories, the story goes that it was in fact built out of spite instead of a promised road, when the constituents of the area failed to elect Paxton as their MP in 1802.

## Talley Abbey

MAP P.81

Talley, Llandeilo, SA19 7YY. www.cadw.gov. wales/visit/places-to-visit/talley-abbey. 24h. Free.

It's worth making a quick stop in the small village of Talley to explore the ruins of Talley Abbey, built in the late twelfth century and surviving until Henry VIII's dissolution of the monasteries. Next to the abbey is St Michael's church, built largely from stones from the abbey, and just outside the churchyard is a pair of small lakes which are a pleasant setting for a short amble.

## Dolaucothi Gold Mine

MAP P.81

Pumsaint, Llanwrda, SA19 8US. 01558 650177, www.nationaltrust.org.uk/ dolaucothi. May–Jul & Sep Wed–Thu & Sun 10am–5pm, Aug Wed–Sun 10am–5pm. £10.

The only known Roman gold mine in Britain, Dolaucothi makes for a fascinating visit as you explore the mine shafts and learn the techniques the Romans used. Roman jewellery fashioned from the gold extracted here is now on display in the British Museum, but it seems that after the Roman period there were no efforts to exploit the gold deposits here until 1872. There are pleasant wooded paths around the estate if you fancy a walk after visiting the mine.

## Carreg Cennen

MAP P.81

Near Trapp, Llandeilo, SA19 6UA. 01558 822291, www.carregcennencastle.com. Daily Apr–Oct 9.30am–6pm, Nov–Mar 9.30am–4pm. £5.50.

The picturesque ruin of Carreg Cennen, found on a lonely hilltop at the western end of the Brecon Beacons National Park, has to be one of the most dramatically situated castles in Wales. Its inhabitants would have had a clear view of anyone approaching from any direction, making it a vital stronghold for the English in their efforts to subjugate the Welsh in the fourteenth century. Much of the walls remain intact, but most inner buildings are largely ruined.

Perhaps the castle's most unusual feature, though, is the long tunnel that plunges deep beneath the castle from a passage in the southeast corner. Indulge your Famous Five fantasies by following this down until it culminates in a dank cave – take the time to check out the gradually calcifying graffiti, some of which dates back to the nineteenth century, before turning your torch off and experiencing total darkness. Mind your head and your step down here – the ceiling is low and the floor is slippery.

The castle makes a great juping-off point for local walks, and there's a small shop and tearoom on site to help replenish your energy.

Newton House on the Dinefwr Estate

# Shops

## Cardigan Guildhall Market

MAP P.78

Guildhall, Cardigan, SA43 1JL. 01239
615554, www.cardigan-guildhall-market.
co.uk. Mon–Sat 9am–5pm.

Cardigan's 'modern Gothic'
Guildhall Market is a busy
collection of stalls selling souvenirs,
textiles, art and antiques. Don't
miss the Syrian food stall, at
which you can pick up a variety of
excellent Middle Eastern treats.

## Crafters Cwtch

MAP P.78

11 Pendre, Cardigan, SA43 1JL. 07837
595556, www.facebook.com/crafterscwtch.
Mon–Tue & Sat 10am–4pm, Wed
10am–5pm, Thu–Fri 10am–3pm.

Souvenir shop on Cardigan's main
shopping drag, where you can pick
up plenty of locally hand-crafted
items such as art, jewellery and
cushions. The back room has some
lovely slate kitchenware.

## National Wool Museum Gift Shop

MAP P.78

Dre-fach Felindre, near Newcastle Emlyn,
SA44 5UP. 0300 1112333, www.museum.
wales/wool. Tue–Sat 10am–5pm.

Not surprisingly, the Wool
Museum's gift shop focuses on
wool ware – there are fine throws
and cushions on sale here, plus
plenty of knitting supplies for you
to make your own products at
home. There's a small selection of
other souvenirs too, mostly of the
edible kind.

# Cafés

## The Owl and the Pussycat

MAP P.80

3 Grist Square, Laugharne, SA33 4SS.
01994 427742, www.facebook.com/
Owl-Pussycat-Tearooms-and-Restaurant-
Laugharne-184539108294915. Thu–Tue
10am–4pm.

Just opposite Laugharne's castle, the
Owl and the Pussycat is a nice little
café that's a convenient spot for
lunch, or simply coffee and a cake.
The Welsh cakes are particularly
recommended.

## Stwdio 3

MAP P.78

3 High St, Cardigan, SA43 1HJ. 01239
758088, www.makeitinwales.co.uk/
stiwdio-3. Mon–Sat 10am–4pm.

This cosy coffee shop on
Cardigan's high street is a great
place for a coffee and cake, or an
excellent lunch. The chocolate
caramel shortbread is crazily
indulgent – it's more caramel than
shortbread, and comes topped
with a flake and caramel sauce.
Stwdio 3 doubles as a small craft
shop – make sure to check out
the enormous knitted "Cardigan
for Cardigan" which hangs in the
stairway.

## Time For Tea

MAP P.80

7 Bridge St, Kidwelly, SA17 4UU.
01554 892908, www.facebook.com/
timeforteakidwelly. Tue–Fri 9.30am–
3.30pm, Sat–Sun 10am–3pm.

A small and friendly café that's
a great choice for lunch after
visiting Kidwelly Castle – the
sandwiches and paninis are
excellent, there are very good
all-day breakfasts for those with
larger appetites, and there's also a
fine selection of cakes if you're just
after a coffee and a snack.

# Restaurants

## 1176

MAP P.78

Cardigan Castle, Green St, SA43 1JA. 01239
562002, www.cardigancastlecom. Daily
8.30am–4pm, plus Fri & Sat 6–9pm.

Elegant, glass café/restaurant
overlooking the castle's gardens on
one side and the Teifi on the other
– though the setting's not the only
reason to visit. Come for breakfast

Cardigan Guildhall

(until 11am), a spot of lunch (including Welsh rarebit and tasty savoury tarts) or, on Friday and Saturday evenings, an unbeatably juicy steak.

## Cofio Lounge

MAP P.80

The Guildhall, Carmarthen, SA31 1PR. 01267 220470, www.thelounges.co.uk/ cofio. Sun–Wed 9am–11pm, Thu–Sat 9am–midnight.

Housed in Carmarthen's old courthouse – head upstairs to peep through internal windows at the original court room – this unexpectedly stylish spot is now decorated wall-to-wall with artwork, and the ceiling is adorned with a huge number of shabby-chic lampshades. There's a good range of food, focussing largely on an extravagant array of burgers, but also running to tapas and sandwiches, as well as an extensive brunch menu.

## El Salsa

MAP P.78

Pwllhai, Cardigan, SA43 1DB. 01239 613705, www.elsalsa.co.uk. Fri–Sat 4.30pm–8.30pm.

This little place has limited opening hours, so make sure you seize the chance to get down to El Salsa when they're open to indulge in some of their excellent Mexican street food. The beef birria burritos are utterly fantastic, and there are some amazing tequila-based cocktails to be had here too. Takeaway only, but there is outdoor seating so you won't have to take your food far.

## Pizzatipi

MAP P.78

1 Cambrian Quay, SA43 1EZ. 01239 612259, www.pizzatipi.co.uk. June–Sept daily noon–9.30pm.

Run by four brothers and a band of their merry friends, the main reason to visit this easy-going waterside café is to dine on sumptuous wood-fired pizza and Welsh craft beer under the ingeniously conceived pizza tepee while gazing out over the river. They also serve delicious sweets and coffee – so it's wise to save room if you can! – and occasionally host the live music and events which are a real treat if you're lucky enough to catch one!

### The Warren

MAP P.80

11 Mansel St, SA31 1PX. 01267 236079, www.warrenmanselst.co.uk. Tue–Wed 10am–4pm, Thurs–Sat 11am–11pm & 6–9.30pm, Sun 10am–4pm.

This laidback, family-run café-bar promises craft beers and gins galore, as well as interesting starters such as spiced Moroccan carrot dip or courgette and kale fritters, and mains from veggie burgers to rump steak with Jerusalem artichoke. The café runs entirely on renewable energy, and also hosts live music nights on the first Sunday of the month.

# Pubs

### Angel Inn

MAP P.81

Salem, Llandeilo, SA19 7LY. 01558 822982, www.theangelinnsalem.co.uk. Thu–Fri noon–3pm & 5pm–10pm, Sat noon–midnight, Sun noon–5pm.

A lovely cosy local pub in the village of Salem, a few miles north of Llandeilo, the Angel is an ideal place to stop for a meal after a day exploring the National Botanic Garden, Carreg Cennan or Dinefwr. The menu includes all the usual pub classics, and there are usually some interesting specials on offer. Rather surprisingly, in one corner is a stuffed grizzly bear called Hugo which was apparently given to the ninth Baron Dinefwr by the poet Dylan Thomas.

### The Daffodil Inn

MAP P.78

Penrhiw-llan, Llandysul, SA44 5NG. 01559 370343, www.daffodilinn.co.uk. Wed–Thu noon–3pm & 5pm–10.30pm, Fri–Sat noon–3pm & 5pm–10.30pm, Sun 11.45am–6pm.

It's worth a detour to the village of Penrhiw-llan to eat at the Daffodil Inn, which thoroughly deserves its Michelin listing and the many awards it has won for its fantastic local food. The slow-roasted lamb belly with baba ghanoush and fcta (£16) is absolutely sublime. There's a brilliant wine list too, and a good selection of Welsh beers on draught to choose from. The wooden terrace outside is the ideal spot to enjoy your meal and offers beautiful valley views.

Seafood at The Daffodil Inn

# ACCOMMODATION

Monkton Old Hall

# Accommodation

There's a huge range of accommodation available in Pembrokeshire, from top class hotels through to lovely B&Bs and excellent camping options. By and large, for family holidays, self-catering places may be the best choice: there are plenty of excellent cottages to be found out in the countryside, and holiday apartments in villages and towns. Families may also enjoy the opportunity to go glamping in yurts, shepherds' huts or pods. Those on a budget will find several youth hostels in the county; the one at Strumble Head in particular has a perfect location. If you prefer your home comforts, you'll be sure to find something to suit from the vast selection of great B&Bs, and for those seeking a memorable stay, there's an almost disproportionate number of swish hotels to be found in Pembrokeshire.

The prices we quote for hotels, guesthouses and B&Bs in this Guide generally refer to the cheapest available double room in high season (usually August), including breakfast, unless otherwise stated. Prices are, predictably, much higher in the summer and school holidays; remember that, in many cases, you'll get the cheapest price if you contact properties directly, rather than booking through agents or websites.

## St Davids and around

**BANK HOUSE** MAP P.24. Whitchurch Road, Solva, SA62 6TR. 01437 721552, www.bankhousesolva.co.uk. There aren't many rooms at Bank House B&B, so you'll need to get in quick if you want to secure your stay at this lovely seventeenth-century cottage in the attractive village of Solva. Beds are comfortable, breakfasts are fantastic, and the hosts have great local knowledge. It's only a short walk down to the village centre, and the coastal path is easily accessible. **£110**

**CRUG GLÂS** MAP P.24. Abereiddy Rd, Solva, St Davids, SA62 6XX. 01348 831302, www.crug-glas.co.uk. Enjoy a touch of Georgian elegance with a stay at this gorgeous old mansion hotel, set in splendid isolation in the countryside close to Abereiddy. The five rooms have been decorated in Georgian and Victorian style, and the bathrooms are magnificently indulgent with freestanding baths. There's a great restaurant too, making this a marvellous place to come to get away from it all. **£160**

**NEWGALE CAMPSITE** MAP P.24. Newgale, SA62 6AS. 07539 906611, www.newgalecampsite.co.uk. The popular campsite on Newgale's seafront has a lot going for it: there's plenty of pitching space for tents, clean toilets and showers, and best of all, a very fine beach just metres away. Catering is available too, with wood-fired pizzas on offer and the Duke of Edinburgh Inn only a short distance off site. The downside is that it's not far from the road, which – although not exactly Piccadilly Circus – can be noisy. **£20**

**RAMSEY HOUSE** MAP P.24 Lower Moor, St Davids, SA62 6RP. 01437 720321, www.ramseyhouse.co.uk. A friendly and welcoming B&B just outside St Davids town centre, Ramsey House has six stylishly decorated rooms with fantastically comfy beds; those upstairs have great views either to the sea or the cathedral. The breakfasts are delicious, consisting almost entirely of locally sourced ingredients, and packed lunches can be provided if you're planning a full day's outing. **£135**

**ST DAVIDS KITCHEN** MAP P.26. 16 Nun St, St Davids, SA62 6NS. 01437 720404, www.stdavidskitchen.co.uk. In the heart of St Davids, this B&B above the popular St Davids Kitchen restaurant offers well-decorated rooms and a great breakfast, but the real draw is the lovely sun terrace which treats you to fabulous views over the town and cathedral across to St Davids Head. It's an absolutely perfect place to watch the sunset. **£140**

**TWR-Y-FELIN** MAP P.26. St Davids, SA62 6QT. 01437 725555, www.twryfelinhotel.com. On the edge of town close to Caerfai Beach, this arty hotel in a former windmill has no less than 41 lovely rooms, some with balconies and most with beautiful views. For real indulgence, check yourself into the Windmill Tower suite and enjoy the 360 degree panorama from your very own observatory. The attached Blas restaurant, which is decorated with slightly odd portraits of Welsh celebrities, offers utterly splendid locally-sourced food. In high season, there's a two-night minimum stay. **£230**

**WHITESANDS HOLIDAY COTTAGES** MAP P.26. Caerbwdi, Bron-y-Graig, St Davids, SA62 6PS. www.whitesandscottages.co.uk/cottages.html. These three self-catering cottages sit in a fantastically privileged position, directly above the magnificent beach of Whitesands Bay – it's a mere ten-minute wander down to the beach. The cottages (which respectively sleep six, eight and nine) are well-appointed, with good kitchens and bedrooms, and wood-burning stoves for colder days. In high season, you'll need to stay for a minimum of one week. **£1180** for one week

# Haverfordwest and around
**THE CLOCK HOUSE** MAP P.34. Marloes, SA62 3AZ. 01646 635800, www.clockhousemarloes.co.uk. This lovely B&B is conveniently situated in the centre of Marloes village, meaning you won't have to travel too far to get to one of the county's best beaches. There are three rooms available, and breakfast is excellent. The Clock House café downstairs is perfect for lunch. **£75**

**THE COUNTY HOTEL** MAP P.34. Salutation Square, Haverfordwest, SA61 2NB. 01437 762144, www.countyhotelhaverfordwest.co.uk. Slap bang in the centre of Haverfordwest, with easy access to the town's restaurants and pubs, the County Hotel is one of the best places to stay if you want to be in the thick of things. Rooms aren't huge but after an extensive refurbishment in 2021, they are smartly decorated, and the staff are very friendly. If you're a light sleeper, ask for a room at the back. **£70**

**FLOATEL** MAP P.34. Nelson Quay, Milford Haven, SA73 3AF. 01646 796176, www.milfordwaterfront.co.uk/whats-here/places-to-stay/floatel-cabins. Whatever will they think of next? These floating cabins, moored in the harbour at Milford Haven and described as a "luxury glamping experience in your very own floating hotel room", are easily one of the quirkiest places to stay in Pembrokeshire. But it's not just a gimmick: with balconies, floor to ceiling windows so you can gaze out at the water, and lovely comfy beds, the Floatel cabins are a genuinely enjoyable experience. **£90**

**MONK HAVEN MANOR** MAP P.34. St Ishmaels, SA62 3TH. 01646 636216, www.monkhaven.co.uk. An off-the-beaten-track B&B just outside the small village of St Ishmaels, Monk Haven Manor was once the vicarage for the adjacent church. It has six lovely rooms and serves up delicious breakfasts, and it's only a short walk down to the small and pebbly but very pretty beach of Monk Haven, from which you can pick up attractive sections of the coastal path. Monk Haven Manor also offers an eco shepherd's hut, which is in a great isolated spot higher up the valley. From **£90**

**THE OLD COASTGUARD COTTAGE** MAP P.34. St Ann's Head, Dale, SA62 3RT. www. theoldcoastguardcottage.com. If you're looking for a splendidly isolated spot for a self-catering getaway, the Old Coastguard Cottage – on the southern tip of St Ann's Head, a short walk from the lighthouse – is a very good choice. The cottage, which sleeps up to eight, is tastefully decorated and has a very well-equipped kitchen, as well as a wood burner for colder evenings. It's a great place to base yourself for coastal walks and visits to the marvellous beaches in this area. From **£880** for one week

**PENDYFFRYN MANOR BED & BREAKFAST** MAP P.34 . Settlands Hill, Little Haven, SA62 3UF. 01437 781863, www. pendyffryn-guesthouse.co.uk. With an enviable location overlooking Little Haven village, Pendyffryn Manor is an excellent B&B offering comfortable bedrooms and a delicious breakfast, as well as a lovely terrace on which you can sit and enjoy the marvellous views. **£105**

**ROCKSDRIFT APARTMENTS** MAP P.34. Enfield Road, Broad Haven, SA62 3JW. 01437 781507, www.broad-haven. com. These well-appointed self-catering apartments on the seafront at Broad Haven are a perfect place for families to stay. The beds are comfy, the kitchen facilities are great, and the owners supply a welcome pack of local goodies. The location can't be faulted either: just across the road from the beach, you'll be able to watch a beautiful sunset right from the window. From **£695** for one week

**ST DAVID'S GUEST HOUSE** MAP P.34. Church Way, Prendergast, Haverfordwest, SA61 2BJ. 01437 766778, www. stdavidsguesthouse.com. This guest house in a former vicarage at the northern end of Haverfordwest is an absolute gem. Friendly, welcoming hosts, excellent breakfasts and a convenient location all combine to make St David's a great place to stay. The Grade II listed property is of Victorian construction, and all rooms have been decorated elegantly to match the house's age – the top choice is the Picton suite, with its marvellous four poster bed. **£100**

**SLATE MILL LODGE** MAP P.34. B4327, near Dale, SA62 3QR. 01646 636767, www. slatemilllodge.co.uk. In a quiet spot near Dale, the Slate Mill Lodge is a fourteenth century corn mill now lovingly converted to offer two self-catering accommodation apartments, each sleeping four people. There's easy access from here to some of the county's best beaches, but the apartments are so relaxing you may find yourself just chilling here instead. Two-night minimum stay. From **£130** a night

## Pembroke and around

**ARCH BARN** MAP P.41. St Twynnels, near Stackpole, SA71 5EE. 01437 765765, www.archbarn.co.uk. This beautiful granary barn conversion, found just ten minutes' drive south of Pembroke, is a great place to stay for a self-catering break. The kitchen is well-appointed and the bedrooms are lovely and comfortable, with the barn's original period features giving the place a fantastic rustic charm. Three-night minimum stay, from **£300**

**EATON HOUSE BED & BREAKFAST** MAP P.44. 108 Main St, Pembroke, SA71 4HN. 01646 831011, www.eatonhousepembroke. co.uk. In a convenient location in Pembroke town centre, Eaton House is a welcoming B&B in a Georgian town house, with just two rooms. The beds are comfortable, the breakfasts are good, and the hosts are full of great advice for your stay. **£80**

**LAMPHEY COURT** MAP P.41. Lamphey, SA71 5NT. 01646 672273, www. lampheycourt.co.uk. A stone's throw from the Bishop's Palace, Lamphey Court is a gorgeous Georgian mansion now converted into an excellent hotel and spa. Rooms are smartly if not particularly imaginatively decorated, the on-site restaurant offers tasty food, and there's a good range of spa treatments available. **£105**

**MONKTON OLD HALL** MAP P.44. 5 Church Terrace, Monkton, Pembroke SA71 4LN. www.landmarktrust.org.uk/search-and-book/properties/monkton-old-hall-9444/#Overview. While not for explorers on a tight budget, this one-of-a-kind self-catering place located in the heart of Pembroke is aptly named: it's thought to possibly date back 600 years and is likely to have been built as a guest house for travellers staying at Monkton Priory. It's been restored multiple times over the centuries and now has all mod cons, but retains a marvellously atmospheric medieval feel. Four-night minimum stay, from **£1800**

**THE ROCKET CART HOUSE** MAP P.41. B4320, near Angle, SA71 5AH. www. coastalcottages.co.uk/cottages/the-rocket-carthouse/?ref=42713. This distinctive self-catering house, complete with a shiny white lookout tower, was once the base for the coastguard rescue team. It's now decorated beautifully with a naval theme and boasts stupendous views across the Angle peninsula and out to sea, especially if you head up onto the roof terrace. Note that the bedrooms in the tower are accessed by fixed wooden ladders. Three-night minimum stay, from **£445**

**STACKPOLE INN** MAP P.41. Jasons Corner, Stackpole, SA71 5DF. 01646 672324, www.stackpoleinn.co.uk. The Stackpole Inn is a lovely village pub with several stylishly decorated rooms; it's a great place to base yourself for a couple of days while exploring the southwest corner of Pembrokeshire. Evening meals at the pub are excellent, so make sure you eat here at least once during your stay. **£125**

**STACKPOLE UNDER THE STARS** MAP P.41. Cheriton,Stackpole, SA71 5BX. 01646 683167, www. stackpoleunderthestars.wales. This lovely campsite offers the opportunity for both camping and glamping: there are several pitches available for tents and campervans, while also on site are a couple of fantastic yurts and a luxury glamping pod. Either way, you'll have access to a fire pit for barbecues, and there's a small shop here for any essentials. A little more unusually, there's also the chance to try your hand at axe throwing on the tomahawk range. **£23** for tent pitching, **£115** for a yurt

# Tenby and around
**AMROTH CASTLE BEACH RESORT** MAP

P.49. Amroth, SA67 8NN. 01834 813217, www.amrothcastle.com. Right on Amroth's seafront, the Castle Beach Resort offers self-catering accommodation in cottages, apartments and even luxury caravans. Amroth Castle itself – a grand nineteenth-century building with a chequered history – stands in the centre of the grounds, and there's also a heated outdoor swimming pool, playground, games room and woodland trail on site, though it's probably the excellent beach that'll prove the top attraction. From **£500** for one week

**CAREW INN** MAP P.49. Bird's Lane, Carew, SA70 8SL. 01646 651267, www. carewinn.co.uk/accommodation.html. A pair of cottages adjacent to the excellent Carew Inn are available as both serviced and self-catering accommodation. These are lovely old buildings, with fantastic character – the beamed ceilings in the first cottage are beautiful – and offer excellent views over the mill pond and castle. **£110**

**CROYLAND GUEST HOUSE** MAP P.51. 10 Deer Park, Tenby, SA70 7LE. 01834 843880, www.thecroyland.co.uk. The welcoming Croyland Guest House has seven ensuite bedrooms, decorated with stylish exposed brickwork. Breakfasts are great, and it's within a very short stroll of the town centre, so there's easy access to the beaches and restaurants. The owners can make great recommendations for local activities and places to eat. **£85**

**ESPLANADE HOTEL** MAP P.51. 1 The Esplanade, Tenby, SA70 7DU. 01834 842760, www.esplanadehoteltenby.com. There's a row of fine old hotels on Tenby's Esplanade overlooking the south beach, but the Esplanade Hotel is the pick of the bunch. The owners are friendly and welcoming, breakfasts are good, and naturally the sea views are outstanding. **£90**

**MANORBIER CASTLE HOUSE** MAP P.49. Manorbier, SA70 7SY. 01834 870081, www. manorbiercastle.co.uk/stay. Ever fancied staying in your own castle? This cosy self-catering cottage inside the walls of Manorbier Castle will give you the chance to fulfil all your medieval fantasies, offering you the run of the fortress for the night.

There's space for 12 people to stay. It's by no means cheap, though. From **£1000** a night

**PARK HOTEL** MAP P.51. North Cliffe, Tenby, SA70 8AT. 01834 842480, www. parkhoteltenby.com. With attractively decorated rooms, excellent views over Tenby's North Beach, and a heated outdoor swimming pool, the Park Hotel is a very solid accommodation choice. There's also direct access to the beach from the hotel grounds and it's only a short walk into town. Unusually for Tenby, there's a large car park on site too. **£160**

**PENALLY ABBEY HOTEL** MAP P.49. Penally, near Tenby, SA70 7PY. 01834 843033, www.penally-abbey.com. A lovely boutique hotel, with cosy rooms offering great views across the nearby coast, Penally Abbey is set in attractive grounds and also has a highly regarded restaurant on site. It's a dog-friendly place, to the extent that there's a dining room specifically set up so you can eat with your canine companion. **£100**

**SEA BREEZE BEACH HOUSE** MAP P.49. Manorbier, SA70 7SX. 01834 871587, www.manorbieraccommodation.co.uk. Sea Breeze Beach House is a self-catering cosy eco cabin with a Scandinavian feel to its design. There's everything you could need here: bed, ensuite, kitchen facilities, barbecue, sun loungers and a log burner. The cabin even has a sky dome in its ceiling so you can see the night sky from the bed. Just ten minutes' walk from the beach and Manorbier village, it's an ideal place for a romantic getaway. Four-night minimum stay in high season, from **£520**

**ST BRIDES SPA HOTEL** MAP P.49. St Brides Hill, Saundersfoot, SA69 9NH. 01834 812304, www.stbridesspahotel. com. Occupying a perfect position on the top of the cliffs above Saundersfoot, the St Brides Spa Hotel is an upmarket place with tastefully decorated rooms, some with balconies overlooking the sea. There's a lovely restaurant on site, the spa facilities are excellent, and best of all, there's an infinity pool with marvellous views looking down towards the beach. **£200**

# Narberth and around

**32 TOWNHOUSE** MAP P.57. 32 High St, Narberth, SA67 7AS. 01834 218338, www.32townhouse.com. Lovely boutique B&B in the heart of Narberth, housed in an attractive Georgian town house. Some of the tastefully decorated rooms have views of the town hall, while others look out over the countryside to the rear. Downstairs, and also run by the B&B's owners, is the popular Top Joe's pizza restaurant. **£130**

**BLUESTONE** MAP P.58. Canaston Wood, near Narberth, SA67 8DE. 01834 862400, www.bluestonewales.com. Ideal for families, this holiday park of attractive self-catering lodges is well-situated for exploring the county, and also boasts a swimming pool and a range of onsite activities, including paddleboarding, archery, and glow-in-the-dark bowling. It's very close to the Oakwood theme park too, so you can ensure the adrenaline never lets up. Four-night minimum stay, from **£749**

**THE GROVE** MAP P.58. Molleston, Narberth, SA67 8BX. 01834 860 915, www. thegrove-narberth.co.uk. One of Wales' most luxurious hotels, the Grove is thought to date back to the 1680s, though it's been extended and modified several times since then, particularly in the 1870s when it acquired a touch of the Victorian craze for Gothic styling. It's a marvellous place for a romantic escape, with a fantastic onsite restaurant, spa treatments available and lovely grounds to explore. Definitely worth a splurge. **£248**

**THE LITTLE RETREAT** MAP P.58. Lawrenny, SA68 0PW. 07973 373833, www. littleretreats.co.uk. Tucked away in the quiet village of Lawrenny on the eastern banks of the Cleddau is this fantastic glamping place, dotted with luxury domes – each with their own hot tub, bathroom and kitchen – and a specially dedicated stargazer tent with transparent panels that's perfect for observing the heavens in this dark sky zone. The Little Retreat can organise activities including wild swimming and paddleboarding, and there's great locally sourced food available on site too. **£220**

**LONGLANDS FARM COTTAGES** MAP P.58. Longlands Farm, Wiston, SA62 4QB. 01437 731313, www.longlandsfarmcottages.co.uk. There are three delightful self-catering cottages here at Longlands, each accommodating four or five people. The buildings may date back as far as the 1600s, but have been sympathetically brought up to date and are equipped with all mod cons. There's a games room onsite too, and the welcome pack including homemade Welsh cakes and eggs fresh from the farm is a lovely touch. From **£775** for one week

**SLEBECH PARK ESTATE** MAP P.58. The Rhos, near Haverfordwest, SA62 4AX. 01437 752000, www.slebech.co.uk. Set in 700 acres of private grounds on the banks of the Cleddau, the Slebech Park Estate is the perfect place to get away. The hotel itself is a former Georgian country mansion, and many of the rooms have been fitted out with gorgeous, slightly offbeat, décor: the two Dunlace rooms in particular are lovely. Exploring the estate grounds is worthwhile: there are very pleasant paths along the riverside and through woodlands to follow, with the chance of seeing wildlife including birds of prey and otters. **£99**

# Fishguard and around

**CRANOG BED & BREAKFAST** MAP P.65. 1 Abercastle Road, Trefin, SA62 5AR. 01348 831507. This lovely B&B in the village of Trefin makes an excellent base for exploring the northern Pembrokeshire coast, with easy access to the coastal path between Abercastle and Porthgain. The breakfasts are delicious and the interior decoration is rather stylish. There are only three rooms, so you may need to be quick to nab one. **£100**

**FFYNNON GRON** MAP P.65. Off B4330, near Letterston, SA62 5QD. 02081 234624, www.ffynnongron.com. This huge sixteenth century farmhouse has been converted to offer self-catering accommodation for up to 16 people, so it's a great place for a big family getaway. Facilities include a well-equipped games room, a barbecue, plenty of outdoor space, and a wood-burning stove for colder evenings. It's within easy reach

of Fishguard, and it's just a short 15-minute drive to the beach at Newgale. Seven-night minimum stay, from **£2500**

**MANOR TOWN HOUSE** MAP P.65. Main St, Fishguard, SA65 9HG. 01348 873260, www.manortownhouse.com. Manor Town House B&B has a seal of approval from no less a traveller than Bill Bryson himself. Four of the six rooms here have a sea view across Fishguard Bay, and all six are attractively decorated, with a mix of antique and modern furniture. Breakfasts are fantastic, and the B&B is in a very convenient spot in the town centre. **£125**

**TREFECHEN WEN** MAP P.65. Llanwnda, Goodwick, SA64 0HS. 07940 334457, www.trefechanwen.com. The two cottages onsite at Trefechen Wen are the converted dairy and barn of a farm, and they retain their rustic character despite modernisation – the interior of the dairy cottage is beautifully stylish. The hosts are genuinely friendly, and there's a great welcome pack included, containing plenty of locally-sourced treats. Each cottage sleeps up to five people, making them ideal for a family self-catering getaway. Two-night minimum stay in high season, from **£340**

**TREGOES** MAP P.65. Manorowen Road, Tregroes, SA65 9QF. 07971 328264, www.tregroes.co.uk. If you're looking to stay in the great outdoors, Tregoes offers plenty of options: alongside pitches for tents and caravans, there are also glamping choices such as self-contained yurts and pods. Fire pits and stoves are available if you want to do your own cooking, or there's a lovely little café on site. Three-night minimum stay in high season. Camping pitch **£25**, glamping **£120** per night

**WOLFSCASTLE COUNTRY HOTEL** MAP P.65. Wolf's Castle, SA62 5LZ. 01437 741225, www.wolfscastle.com. For a touch of luxury, book yourself a night or two in the Wolfscastle Country Hotel. The rooms are smart, the onsite restaurant is deservedly popular, and there's a full range of spa facilities. Wolf's Castle is a small village that's equally convenient for Haverfordwest and Fishguard. **£103**

**YHA PWLL DERI** MAP P.65. Castell Mawr, Trefasser, SA64 0LR. 0345 3719536, www. yha.org.uk/hostel/pwll-deri. Splendidly located self-catering hostel (4 miles west of Goodwick and the nearest shops), with en-suite dorms and a couple of private twin rooms. It's also available for private hire if you're a larger party. The views out to sea from here are marvellous, and it's perfect for walking the Strumble Head cliff path or climbing Garn Fawr. Closed Oct–Mar. Dorms **£18**, twins **£49**

# Newport and around

**BETHSAIDA** MAP P.70. High St, St Dogmaels, SA43 3EQ. 01239 615749, www.bethsaida.wales. This former Baptist chapel – much of which remains in situ (the pulpit functions as the reception desk) – has been brilliantly converted into a top-drawer guesthouse, hosting five stunningly original rooms; stained-glass windows, pre-loved furnishings and pew headboards are just a few of its fine original features. Breakfast, meanwhile, is taken in the dining area (the old organ space) behind the pulpit or, when it's warmer, on the pretty garden terrace. **£99**

**CNAPAN GUEST HOUSE** MAP P.70. East St, Newport, SA42 0SY. 01239 820575, www.cnapan.co.uk. This great B&B in the centre of Newport offers five lovely rooms, all smartly decorated, and many of them with beautiful views over St Mary's Church and across to the slopes of Carn Ingli. There's a very pleasant and secluded garden at the rear which is perfect for relaxing in, and the breakfasts are excellent, with a classic full Welsh option alongside some great vegetarian choices. Also on site is a separate self-catering cottage, ideal for up to six people. **£105**

**CWM CONNELL COASTAL COTTAGES** MAP P.70. Moylegrove, SA43 3BX. 01239 881691, www.cwmconnell.co.uk. Tucked away in the countryside, near the remote Ceibwr Bay, this collection of six self-catering cottages – sleeping between two and six people – offers a perfect chance to get away from it all. There's easy access to some of Pembrokeshire's most beautiful and rugged coast path from here,

and to relax in style in the evenings there's a hot tub and sauna on site. From **£640** for one week

**LLYS MEDDYG** MAP P.70. East St, Newport, SA42 0SY. 01239 820008, www. llysmeddyg.com. Comfy-chic restaurant-with-rooms fashioned from a Georgian coaching inn, displaying fine local art. All rooms have great bedding, classy toiletries and individual décor, and some have lovely free-standing bathtubs. Dogs are welcome in several rooms – check the website for details. The food at the restaurant is good, too. **£120**

**NEWPORT LINKS GOLF CLUB** MAP P.70. Golf Course Rd, Newport, SA42 0NR. 01239 820244, www.newportsands.co.uk. If you're wanting easy access to Newport's excellent beach, you won't find a better spot than Newport Links – it'll take you just five minutes to walk down onto the sand. The rooms are comfortable, and there are lovely views over the sea. The restaurant isn't always open in the evenings, so check with staff beforehand if you're planning to eat here. **£110**

**RHOSTWARCH** MAP P.70. Brynberian, Crymych, SA41 3TG. 01239 891637, www. rhostwarch.co.uk. High in the peaceful Preseli Hills, Rhostwarch is a B&B with four en-suite rooms with a slightly rustic feel, offering great locally-sourced breakfasts. There's also a self-catering farmhouse on site, which sleeps up to ten people. The hot tub is a godsend for relaxing after long walks in the hills. **£85**

**TEIFI NETPOOL INN** MAP P.70. St Dogmaels, SA43 3ET. 01239 612680, www. teifinetpoolinn.com. Each of the seven rooms at this great B&B in St Dogmaels is named after and decorated in a different colour, so make sure to browse the website and choose your favourite when booking. Some rooms also offer lovely views over the Teifi river. The owner is very friendly with great suggestions for local activities, and breakfast is delicious. **£85**

**THE TREWERN ARMS** MAP P.70. Nevern, SA42 0NB. 01239 820395, www. trewernarms.com. The rustic sixteenth-century Trewern Arms is a welcoming pub in Nevern village, with several pleasant and modernised rooms for overnight stays. Breakfasts are very popular, with local goat sausages taking pride of place on the menu. **£95**

## Further afield

**BLACK LION HOTEL** MAP P.78. High St, Cardigan, SA43 1HJ. 01239 612532, www. blacklionhotelcardigan.com. Right in the centre of Cardigan, this pub has an impressively long history – it may have been established as long ago as 1105, and it claims to be the oldest coaching inn in Wales. The rooms are comfy and the breakfasts are good. Given its position on the High Street, it can be noisy at night, so consider a room at the back if you're a light sleeper. **£60**

**BROWNS** MAP P.80. King St, Laugharne, SA33 4RY. 01994 427688, www.browns. wales. Once Dylan Thomas' favourite place for a tipple, Browns is an upmarket hotel that's attracted plenty of famous visitors, including Elizabeth Taylor, Mick Jagger and Pierce Brosnan, and enjoyed a spell under the ownership of Neil Morrissey. Each room is tastefully decorated in its own individual style – our favourites are the lovely rustic Llareggub and Corran. The attached restaurant is excellent. **£150**

**THE CAWDOR** MAP P.81. 70 Rhosmaen St, Llandeilo, SA19 6EN. 01558 823500, www.thecawdor.com. Llandeilo's focal point, this former coaching inn has been given a modern makeover with delightful, simply decorated rooms (all different) and stunning attic suites. It's particularly fun to stay if you're a Lord of the Rings fan, giving you the chance to declare that "One does not simply walk into Cawdor", which never gets old. **£85**

**CLYDEY COTTAGES** MAP P.78. Penrallt, Lancych, Boncath, SA37 0LW. 01239 698619, www.clydeycottages.co.uk. A brilliant place for a family getaway, there are ten rustic eighteenth-century self-catering cottages available here, with capacity for between two and eight guests. There's an indoor swimming pool and regular activities for kids, including feeding the farm animals, and it's surrounded by gorgeous countryside. The only downside is that it's not cheap. One week minimum stay, **£3100**

**THE HIVEAWAY** MAP P.78. Llain, Penrhiwllan, Llandysul. 07534 275209, www.thehiveaway.co.uk. A glamping pod with a difference, the Hiveaway is beautifully decorated with a – you guessed it – honeycomb theme. Set in gorgeous countryside, and well equipped with a wood-fired hot tub, a fire pit, and a stargazing skylight, this is a truly luxurious place to get back to nature without sacrificing home comforts. Highly recommended. **£120**

**PENLAN COASTAL COTTAGES** MAP P.78. Penlan Farm, Aberporth, SA43 2DT. 01239 810442, www.penlancoastalcottages. co.uk. Just out of Aberporth, Penlan Coastal Cottages are lovely self-catering homes with well-appointed kitchens, attractive interior decoration, great views down to the sea, and hot tubs. There's also a gorgeous patio, decked with flowers, that makes the perfect place for al fresco meals. There are four cottages available, sleeping between two and six people each. From **£400** for one week

**THE WELSH REINDEER RETREAT** MAP P.80. Ystradfach Farm, Llandyfaelog, Kidwelly, SA17 5NY. 01269 861376, www. thewelshreindeerretreat.co.uk. The two bed and breakfast rooms at this welcoming place were once the farm's milking parlour, but have been modernised and now exude a lovely rustic charm. There's also a self-catering cottage onsite, which sleeps up to six people, and for those who want to get back to basics, a shepherd's hut is available too. The real draw, of course, are the eponymous reindeer – and the farm's many other animals – who will prove to be a particular hit with kids. Two-night minimum stay, from **£110** a week

# ESSENTIALS

Catching the boat to Ramsey Island

# Arrival

There are a number of routes into Pembrokeshire, though if you're coming by public transport you'll almost certainly arrive into Haverfordwest by train or main road from Cardiff; routes into the north of the county are rather more limited. However you arrive, be prepared: though the journey will be worth it, it's likely to take a while, as this is a fairly remote corner of the UK.

## By car

The majority of visitors to Pembrokeshire arrive by car, and most of these come in along the A40 from Carmarthen. Carmarthen is a four-and-a-half-hour drive from London along the M4, passing Reading, Bristol, Cardiff and Swansea en route. The M4 terminates just past Swansea, from which you'll pick up the A48 to Carmarthen. If coming from the north, though, you may come cross-country on the A483 and A40 from the Midlands, or for a prettier but longer drive you could opt for the A494 through Snowdonia before picking up the coastal A487 past Aberystwyth.

## By coach

National Express coaches (08717 818181, www.nationalexpress.com/en) have one route into Pembrokeshire, with infrequent direct services from London to Haverfordwest (£40 return), though you'll more usually have to change at Cardiff. These services also call at a few other Pembrokeshire destinations, the most useful of which are probably Tenby and Pembroke. To reach the county from the north, TrawsCymru (0300 2002233, www. trawscymru.info) operates a route from Aberystwyth that calls at Fishguard and Haverfordwest (£6.30 single).

## By train

It's possible to reach Pembrokeshire by direct train from as far away as Manchester Piccadilly, which operates services to Milford Haven via Haverfordwest roughly every two hours (taking six and a half hours, £65 return), but most train journeys into the county will involve a change at Cardiff, Swansea or Whitland. Many of the county's towns have a station, including Haverfordwest, Milford Haven, Narberth, Tenby and Pembroke, though note that St Davids does not have a rail link.

## By ferry

If travelling from Ireland, the ferry services from Rosslare are your best bet. You can either sail to Pembroke Dock with Irish Ferries (four hours sailing, from £150 with car) or to Goodwick, just outside Fishguard, with Stena Line (www.stenaline.co.uk, three and a half hours sailing, from £110 with car).

## By air

There's a small airport at Haverfordwest (www.pembrokeshire. gov.uk/haverfordwest-airport), but it's not served by any commercial flights. The nearest airports operating standard commercial flights are Cardiff and Bristol; if travelling by air, it's best to fly into one of these, then make your way to Pembrokeshire by train, coach or car. Cardiff Airport is relatively poorly served with flights from mainland Europe, althought the announcement by WizzAir (www.wizzair.com) that Cardiff will become another of their UK bases should open up more destinations on the continent in future. Bristol Airport (www.bristolairport.co.uk), however, is just across the border and has some excellent connections with mainland Europe.

# Getting around

Pembrokeshire isn't hugely convenient for getting about by public transport; while bus and train links do exist, services aren't enormously frequent, so you'll need to plan carefully. For drivers, the county is criss-crossed by a network of often small roads, and the distances are not great so no journey should take more than an hour. Pembrokeshire is ideal for travelling under your own steam, particularly for walkers who can avail themselves of the fantastic coastal path.

## Driving

The road network around Pembrokeshire is extensive, with good roads connecting all the principal towns, though you won't find many stretches with more than one lane for each direction. The further out of the towns you go, the more likely you are to find single track roads, which can often be bordered by high hedges and inconveniently lacking in passing places, as well as featuring some serious bends – take care on these sections.

It's generally easy to find parking – most beaches have car parks, often operated by the National Trust, and there are plenty of car parks in towns and villages. Usually these charge during the summer only, and generally you can pay either for about three hours or for the whole day.

There are scenic drives all over the county, but perhaps the most visually arresting is the B4329 from Haverfordwest, which from Tufton onwards heads up into the Preseli Hills, affording an absolutely stunning view in all directions from its highest point near the summit of Foel Eryr. There's a car park here so you can stop and admire the scenery.

## Buses

A number of operators, including Edwards Brothers (01437 890230), First (www.firstbus.co.uk/south-west-wales), Taf Valley Coaches (01994 240908) and TrawsCymru (www.trawscymru.info), run services across Pembrokeshire; the full range of routes can be browsed online at www.pembrokeshire.gov.uk/bus-routes-and-timetables. Prices vary between operators; day tickets with unlimited travel are offered by First and TrawsCymru (£4.50 and £11 respectively).

## Bus routes

Particularly useful bus routes include T5 Cardigan – Fishguard – Haverfordwest; T11 Haverfordwest – St Davids – Fishguard; 311 Haverfordwest – Broad Haven; 349 Haverfordwest – Pembroke Dock – Tenby; 351 Pendine – Amroth – Saundersfoot – Tenby; 360 Pembroke Dock – Carew – St Florence – Tenby; 381 Tenby – Narberth – Haverfordwest; 387 Pembroke Dock – Angle – Stackpole; 400 St Davids – Marloes; and 430 Cardigan – Crymych – Narberth. Services aren't hugely frequent; on some routes, such as the 381, they run hourly, but in many cases they're limited to just three or four times a day.

There's also a service called Fflecsi operating in Pembrokeshire (www.fflecsi.wales); using from a free app on your mobile phone, you can request a bus to pick you up and drop you off from anywhere within a specified service area, rather than sticking to bus stops on a standard route. Currently, the three service areas in operation roughly cover a triangle encompassing St Davids, Haverfordwest and Fishguard. Fares start from £4.

## Train

While many of Pembrokeshire's towns have train stations, they're rather frustratingly split into three lines that only connect back at Whitland in Carmarthenshire – so if you wish to take the train from Fishguard to Pembroke, for example, it'll take you an infuriating three and a half hours. Broadly speaking, the most realistic proposition for exploring the county by rail is to use the south coast line which operates a decent service calling at Narberth, Saundersfoot, Tenby, Manorbier and Pembroke. The other two lines allow transit between Haverfordwest and Milford Haven, and Fishguard and Clarbeston Road.

Services are operated by Transport for Wales (www.tfw.wales). Fares are unlikely to exceed £20 no matter where you're travelling within Pembrokeshire, and are usually much lower. Book at least a day in advance online to secure the best prices.

## Cycling

Cycling is a good way of getting around Pembrokeshire, but be aware that many roads are narrow, winding and banked by high hedges, meaning that drivers often won't get much warning that you're there. Terrain is not flat, so you'll find yourself going up and down perhaps more than you'd expect. Also note that dedicated cycle lanes are few and far between, though the one on the Cleddau bridge between Pembroke Dock and Neyland affords excellent views over the river.

You'll find a list of suggested cycle routes of varying distance and difficulty online at www. pembrokeshire.gov.uk/cycle-pembrokeshire, and some family friendly routes are suggested at www. visitpembrokeshire.com/articles/let-the-kids-rip-family-biking. Bikes can be rented from a number of suppliers, including Pembrokeshire Bike Hire (07427 672797, www. pembrokeshirebikehire.co.uk), who offer both standard and e-bikes, and can deliver the bike to your accommodation, depending on where you're staying.

## Walking

Pembrokeshire is a perfect destination for keen walkers; the coast path, which runs for 186 miles along the county's stunning cliffs and beaches, is ideal for casual and long-distance hikers alike. If you're planning on tackling the entire length from Poppit Sands to Amroth or vice versa, you'll need about two weeks, but most people pick and choose particularly attractive sections: our picks for the most scenic parts include the stretch around Stackpole Head, the Marloes peninsula, Abereiddy to Abercastle, and Strumble Head, though strong cases could be made for pretty much any section.

The path involves a fair bit of ascent and descent as you pass various beaches and bays, and is rarely paved, instead usually consisting of grass or dirt tracks. Make sure you have adequate footwear and weather-appropriate clothing, and you might want to consider taking walking poles. If you're walking the whole length and carrying all your gear with you, particularly in high season, it's advisable to book accommodation in advance to save yourself unnecessary effort lugging your backpack around guesthouses trying to find somewhere with an available room.

## Boat trips

The boat trips available in various locations around the county offer a great chance to see Pembrokeshire from an alternative perspective. Usually focussed on the area's excellent wildlife spotting opportunities, these include the Pembrokeshire Islands trips from

Martin's Haven (see page 36) which take you around Skomer, Skokholm and Grassholm, and the Thousand Islands

Expeditions from St Davids (see page 27) around Ramsey Island.

# Directory A-Z

## Children

Pembrokeshire is a perfect destination for children of all ages, with a huge range of activities available. The obvious first port of call is one of the many beautiful sandy beaches: Tenby and Broad Haven are particularly good choices, with easy access to facilities and generally gentle waves making them ideal for paddling. Older children who want to get active on the water will find ample opportunities for bodyboarding at Whitesands, Marloes and Freshwater West.

The county is full of days out that children are guaranteed to enjoy, particularly in the southeast around Tenby and Narberth – Folly Farm, the Dinosaur Park and Oakwood are all great choices – and those with an active imagination will love the many castles, with Pembroke being a particularly fine choice. Museums vary in their efforts to engage kids: Narberth's puts in a good showing, for example, while Tenby's is perhaps best avoided if visiting with children.

Children are almost always welcome at pubs and restaurants, and in most accommodation: check when booking as occasionally B&Bs will not accept anyone under twelve years old. The plentiful self-catering options in Pembrokeshire are perhaps the best choice when holidaying with children.

## Cinema

There are no big multiplexes in Pembrokeshire, but there is a two-screen cinema in Haverfordwest (Upper Market St, Haverfordwest, SA61 1QA. 01437 767675, www.palacehaverfordwest.co.uk) that shows the latest blockbusters. There are combination theatre/cinemas in Fishguard (Theatr Gwaun, West St, Fishguard, SA65 9AD. 01348 873421, www.theatrgwaun.com) and Milford Haven (Torch Theatre, St Peter's Road, Milford Haven, SA73 2BU. 01646 695267, www.torchtheatre.co.uk) where you can see films, theatre productions, and the occasional simulcast of theatre or music events. The Torch Theatre in particular is excellent.

In the summer, you'll occasionally find open air drive-in cinema events: one such can be found at Nolton Haven (01437 710360, www.facebook.com/noltondrivein), which puts on classic films such as *Jurassic Park* and *Star Wars* in a lovely spot overlooking St Brides Bay.

## Crime and emergencies

Pembrokeshire is a generally safe place, but it's always advisable to stay alert. If you need them, you can contact the police, fire brigade, ambulance or coastguard by telephone on 999, or in non-emergency cases 111 (dial 112 for the coastguard).

## Discount passes

A good number of the car parks around the Pembrokeshire coast are owned by the National Trust (www.nationaltrust.org.uk), so if you're a member, you'll be able to use these for free. National Trust members can also visit the Trust's properties, such as the Tudor Merchant's House in Tenby, without charge.

Several other historic properties in the county – including the Bishop's

Palace at St Davids – are operated by Cadw (www.cadw.gov.wales). Entry to these is often free, but where charges apply Cadw members enter free, and English Heritage (www.english-heritage.org.uk) members are entitled to 50 percent off.

Tickets for a couple of other places – such as Cardigan Castle – are valid for up to one year, allowing for repeat visits. Season tickets are available for attractions like Oakwood and Folly Farm, so if you're planning multiple visits, these could represent better value.

## Electricity

The current in Wales is 240V AC. North American appliances will need a transformer and adaptor; those from Europe, South Africa, Australia and New Zealand only need an adaptor.

## Health

Visitors to Pembrokeshire should check current and incoming Covid-19 restrictions for Wales online at www.gov.wales/coronavirus. Pembrokeshire's main hospital, and the only one with an A&E, is Withybush Hospital, just north of Haverfordwest (Fishguard Road, Haverfordwest, SA61 2PZ. 01437 764545, www.hduhb.nhs.wales/healthcare/hospitals-and-centres/hospitals/withybush-hospital), though there are also small community hospitals in Pembroke Dock (Fort Road, Pembroke Dock, SA72 6SY. 01646 682114, www.hduhb.nhs.wales/healthcare/hospitals-and-centres/community-hospitals/south-pembrokeshire-hospital) and Tenby (Gas Lane, Norton, Tenby, Pembrokeshire, SA70 8AG. 01834 845400, www.hduhb.nhs.wales/healthcare/hospitals-and-centres/community-hospitals/tenby-hospital). Doctors and dentists can be found in the towns and some of the larger villages, and pharmacies are easy to come by – there's a list of them covering Pembrokeshire, Ceredigion and Carmarthenshire online at www.wales.nhs.uk/ourservices/directory/hywelddauniversityhealthboard/pharmacies.

## Internet

Signal strength isn't always the most reliable, but by and large you'll be able to access the internet from much of Pembrokeshire. This does not extend to more isolated stretches of the cliff path and down on the beaches. If you're relying on having access to specific information, it's wise to consider downloading offline copies before setting off.

## Left luggage

There are no dedicated left luggage services in Pembrokeshire, but in most cases your accommodation will be happy to hold onto your bags for the day after you've checked out. Those walking the coast path may wish to avail themselves of luggage transportation services such as those offered by Preseli Taxis (01437 764050, www.preselitaxis.co.uk/luggage-transfers) and Clarks Taxis (01437 710077, www.clarkstaxis.co.uk/pembrokeshire-coastpath-luggage-transfers) to transfer your bags between accommodation.

## LGBTQ+ travellers

Pembrokeshire is a generally tolerant place for the LGBTQ+ community, which is in line with the Welsh government's intention to make Wales the most LGBTQ+ friendly nation in Europe, stated in 2021. The nearest major Pride event takes place annually in Cardiff (www.pridecymru.com).

## Lost property

The South Wales police have an interactive online form (www.south-wales.police.uk/ro/report/lp/

lost-or-found-property) to complete if you have lost or found something. The webpage also offers advice on the best course of action.

## Money (including ATMs, banks, costs, credit cards, exchange)

Britain's currency is the pound sterling (£), divided into 100 pence (p). Coins come in denominations of 1p, 2p, 5p, 10p, 20p, 50p, £1 and £2. Notes are in denominations of £5, £10, £20 and £50. Scottish and Northern Irish banknotes are legal tender throughout Britain, though some traders may be unwilling to accept them. £50 notes are also sometimes met with suspicion.

Generally speaking, contactless or chip and pin card payments are accepted everywhere, though in some cases – to pay for some car parks, for example – you're still going to need cash. ATMs and banks can be found in all the towns and a few of the larger villages, but it's always worth having some cash as a backup.

## Opening hours

Shops in Pembrokeshire tend to keep relatively standard business hours, and can generally be relied upon to be open from Monday to Saturday between 10am and 4pm at the least. Pubs and restaurants usually serve food between around noon and 3pm, then again from 6pm to 9pm, though this varies between establishments and depending on whether it's high or low season. Several attractions close entirely over the winter, though most operate year-round with reduced hours between November and March.

## Post offices

You'll find post offices in all the main towns in Pembrokeshire, as well as several villages. Most open Monday to Friday between 9am and 5.30pm, though a few (such as Milford Haven) keep longer hours, from 8am to 8pm daily. Specific branch opening hours can be checked online at www. postoffice.co.uk/branch-finder. If you need stamps, these can be purchased in supermarkets and most village shops as well as post offices.

## Smoking

Smoking is illegal in all indoor public spaces in Pembrokeshire, including public transport, museums, pubs and restaurants. Vaping (e-cigarettes) is not covered by this law, but is banned on public transport, and individual establishments have the right to prohibit it on their premises. If unsure, check with the proprietor.

## Time

Greenwich Mean Time (GMT) – equivalent to Coordinated Universal

## Public holidays

Britain's public holidays (Bank Holidays), are:
January 1
Good Friday
Easter Monday
First Monday in May
Last Monday in May
Last Monday in August
December 25
December 26
Note that if January 1, December 25 or December 26 falls on a Saturday or Sunday, the next weekday becomes a public holiday.

Time (UTC) – is used from the end of October to the end of March; for the rest of the year Britain switches to British Summer Time (BST), one hour ahead of GMT. GMT is five hours ahead of the US Eastern Standard Time and ten hours behind Australian Eastern Standard Time.

## Tipping
There are no specific tipping rules in Pembrokeshire or in Wales as a whole, but staff in restaurants will normally expect a ten to fifteen percent tip. This tends to apply less in pubs and cafés where you pay for your food in advance, though in these places you may find a jar by the till for tips. Note that some bills, usually in the more upmarket places, will add a discretionary service charge for you – you are not obliged to pay this, particularly if you felt the food or service wasn't up to scratch.

## Toilets
Public toilets can be easily found across Pembrokeshire: you'll find them in most car parks at beaches and in towns. There's usually no charge to use them, but occasionally you'll run across one asking for 20p or so.

## Tourist information
There are few dedicated tourist information centres in Pembrokeshire.

One of the best is the Oriel y Parc Gallery & Visitor Centre in St Davids (St Davids, SA62 6NW. 01437 720392, www.pembrokeshirecoast.wales/oriel-y-parc, daily 9.30am–4.30pm), where the knowledgeable staff can help with plans for your visit to Pembrokeshire, particularly in the St Davids area. Oriel y Parc also houses an art gallery, a café, and a good souvenir shop.

Elsewhere in the county, tourist info services operate out of the libraries in Fishguard, Haverfordwest, Milford Haven, Pembroke and Saundersfoot. See www.visitpembrokeshire.com/contact-us for details.

For online information, the Visit Pembrokeshire website (www.visitpembrokeshire.com) is fantastic, with extensive searchable lists of activities, sights, and recommended accommodation and restaurants.

## Travellers with disabilities
Almost all car parks in Pembrokeshire have reserved spaces for visitors with disabilities. Transport for Wales offers accessibility assistance for passengers wishing to use the rail service; there is an intention to introduce a new fleet of trains with improved accessibility by December 2022. Bus services operated by First and TrawsCymru are wheelchair accessible, but advise making contact prior to travel.

# Festivals and events

Pembrokeshire is home to a number of fun events throughout the year, which range from physical challenges, such as the Tour of Pembrokeshire cycling race, through food-focused events like the Pembrokeshire Fish Week, all the way to some excellent arts and music festivals. A non-exhaustive list of events can be found at www.visitpembrokeshire.com/attractions-events/festivals-and-events.

## Tour of Pembrokeshire
**May, www.tourofpembrokeshire.co.uk**
Around 1,500 cyclists complete in a race around northern Pembrokeshire, with four routes of differing levels of difficulty to choose from, ranging between 25 and 105 miles. With the starting line in St Davids, your route may take you up into the Preseli Hills and – for the truly dedicated – all the way down to Dale.

## The Big Retreat

**June, www.thebigretreatfestival.com**
One of the Guardian's picks for best wellbeing and adventure festivals in the UK, the Big Retreat, held in lush green Lawrenny on the banks of the Cleddau, offers a fun musical line-up as well as an eclectic range of other activities, such as lovespoon carving workshops, dance classes, and yoga sessions.

## Unearthed

**June, www.unearthedfestival.co.uk**
Unearthed, held near Solva, is an open-minded festival with the avowed aim of expanding attendees' consciousness. Music is of the reggae, world and folk genres, and you'll also find yoga classes, meditation workshops and tents dedicated solely to chilling out. Come along for a weekend of mind expansion.

## Pembrokeshire Fish Week

**June, www.pembrokeshirefishweek. co.uk/home**
A nine-day celebration of Pembrokeshire's excellent seafood, held in various venues across the county including Milford Haven, Saundersfoot and Fishguard. Events at the festival can include classes in seafood preparation, fish-themed story-telling for the little ones, and lectures on topics such as ocean plastics – but it's first and foremost a great excuse to sample plenty of well-prepared fishy dishes.

## Westival

**July, www.westival.wales**
An intimate music festival held in Manorbier, usually welcoming around 1,500 guests. Expect to see performances from local and international acts, as well as lengthy DJ sets. Provides a useful shuttle bus to the beach.

## Llangwm Literary Festival

**August, www.llangwmlitfest.co.uk**
Llangwm, on the west banks of the Cleddau, plays host to an annual literary festival at which you can enjoy talks from authors, undertake creative writing classes, and view displays of works by local artists. There's also a young persons' writing competition, so get your entries in.

## Ironman Wales

**September, www.ironman.com/ im-wales**
Each September, Tenby plays host to competitors hoping to win the challenging Ironman race, which involves multiple swimming loops around the harbour, a 112-mile cycle ride around the Angle peninsula and up to Narberth, followed by a full 26-mile marathon around Tenby itself. Never mind winning, just managing to complete that lot is a serious achievement.

## Tenby Arts Festival

**September, www.tenbyartsfest.co.uk**
The week-long Tenby Arts Festival is fairly highbrow, featuring piano recitals, theatre performances and talks on diverse topics. It also features temporary art displays in galleries around the town, sometimes with workshops that you can participate in.

## Narberth Food Festival

**September, www. narberthfoodfestival.com**
Narberth Food Festival is an opportunity to sample and purchase a huge range of fantastic local produce, from honey to cheese and meat to ice cream. In between all the eating, there are chef demonstrations and workshops on topics as diverse as foraging and fermentation, and there's also live music to keep you entertained while you nibble.

# Chronology

**250,000 BC** Earliest evidence of human existence in Wales.

**2000 BC** Bronze Age settlers arrive in Wales from the Iberian peninsula.

**c.3000 BC** Neolithic burial chambers such as Pentre Ifan constructed by Pembrokeshire's early inhabitants.

**c.500 BC** Iron Age forts such as Castell Henllys built across Pembrokeshire.

**c.52 AD** Potential first date for the arrival of the Romans, though it's uncertain how much influence Rome had on Pembrokeshire.

**78 AD** Roman conquest of Wales completed as Agricola kills druids of Anglesey.

**c.350 AD** Irish settlers known as the Déisi arrive in Pembrokeshire.

**Early 4th century** Roman departure from Wales.

**c.410** Pembrokeshire becomes part of the newly formed Kingdom of Dyfed, which lasts for 500 years.

**c.500** St David (Dewi Sant) born.

**c.589** St David dies after a life of miracles. He later becomes Wales' patron saint.

**c.800–c.1000** Pembrokeshire subjected to Viking raids. The legacy of the Vikings can still be seen in place names such as Skokholm and Ramsey.

**1067** Normans arrive to begin the conquest of Pembrokeshire.

**c.1100** The collection of Welsh stories known as the *Mabinogion* is compiled,

featuring Narberth as the court of Prince Pwyll.

**1181** Construction of the current St Davids cathedral begins.

**1189** William Marshal, "the greatest knight who ever lived", becomes Earl of Pembroke.

**1191** Gerald of Wales completes his medieval travel guide, *The Journey Through Wales*, giving glowing reviews to Pembrokeshire and particularly Manorbier.

**1328** Henry de Gower becomes Bishop of St Davids; under his tenure, the Bishop's Palace is expanded into a grand residence.

**1405** Owen Glyndwr captures much of Pembrokeshire in his rebellion against the English.

**1416** Owen Glyndwr dies while in hiding.

**1457** Henry Tudor, the future Henry VII, is born at Pembroke Castle.

**1536** Henry VIII establishes Pembrokeshire as a county.

**1588** The complete Bible is translated into Welsh for the first time, chiefly by William Morgan.

**1644** Pembrokeshire is conquered by parliamentarian forces during the English Civil War.

**1780** Landscaping work at the Stackpole Estate results in the creation of Bosherston Lily Ponds.

**1797** French forces land at Fishguard in the "Last Invasion" of Britain.

**1802** Sir William Paxton begins investing in Tenby with the aim of promoting the town as a tourism destination.

**1839–43** Chartists uprising in Newport led by John Frost. Toll gates are destroyed in protests against high taxation in the Rebecca Riots.

**c.1850** Mining on the Pembrokeshire Coalfield is at its peak.

**1860** Work begins on the fortresses eventually to be known as Palmerston's Follies.

**1866** Abermawr beach becomes the eastern terminal of the Transatlantic telegraph cable.

**1914–18** Milford Haven's naval base is active in countering the U-boat threat during World War I.

**1925** Plaid Genedlaethol Cymru (Welsh National Party) formed.

**1926** Miners' strike and General Strike take place in May.

**1940–41** Pembroke Dock is targeted by the Luftwaffe in bombing raids.

**1943** American troops practise for the D-Day landings on beaches such as Saundersfoot.

**1951** Minister for Welsh Affairs appointed.

**1952** Pembrokeshire Coast National Park is established.

**1960** First oil refinery at Milford Haven is opened.

**1967** Welsh Language Act passed. Limited recognition of Welsh as a formal, legal language.

**1970** Pembrokeshire Coastal Path is established.

**1979** The Millennium Falcon for *Star Wars* is constructed at Pembroke Dock.

**1982** Welsh-language TV channel S4C begins broadcasting.

**1992** Welsh Language Bill gives Welsh equal status with English in public bodies.

**1999** First Welsh Assembly elections. Assembly begins sitting.

**1996** The *Sea Empress* runs aground off Milford Haven, causing an oil spill that proves devastating to local wildlife.

**2002** The National Eisteddfod of Wales is held in St Davids; the incoming Archbishop of Canterbury, Rowan Williams, attends and becomes a druid.

**2016** Pembrokeshire votes 57.1% to 42.9% in favour of leaving the EU in the EU Referendum.

**2018** An Iron Age chariot, dating to the first century AD, is discovered by metal detectorist in South Pembrokeshire.

**2020** The Covid-19 outbreak results in a 50% reduction in tourism activity, as well as a national lockdown, school closures and the cancellation of various festivals and events.

**2021** Tenby makes national news when an Arctic walrus called Wally makes the lifeboat slipway his temporary home.

**2022** As of January, 79.1% of Wales' population had received at least one vaccination against Covid-19, with 74.5% of the total population having been double-vaxxed.

# Welsh

After centuries of suppression, the use of Welsh (Cymraeg) is now encouraged, and the number of speakers is increasing. Consequently, it's spoken widely throughout Pembrokeshire, though more commonly in the north of the county; Southern Pembrokeshire is often referred to as 'Little England Beyond Wales', as it is predominately English in both culture and language. The approximate boundary, known as the Landsker Line, runs roughly from Newgale to Laugharne; north of this, you're more likely to find people using Welsh in the first instance, and it's easy to see the dividing line in the names of the settlements.

## The politics of the language

Welsh has survived thanks to those who campaigned to save it, principally the eisteddfod revivalists of the eighteenth century and the political movements of the twentieth century. The formation of Plaid Cymru, the Welsh National Party, in 1925 was largely around the issue of language, as its politics have been ever since. Concerns about the language reached their peak with the 1962 radio broadcast Tynged yr iaith (The Fate of the Language) by the Plaid founder member, Saunders Lewis. This became a rallying cry that resulted in the formation of Cymdeithas yr Iaith Gymraeg, the Welsh Language Society, the following year. One of the highes tprofile early campaigns was the daubing of monoglot English road signs with their Welsh translations. Nearly all signs are now officially in both languages. A 1967 Welsh Language Act allowed many forms of officialdom to be conducted in either language, stating that Welsh, for the first time in more than four hundred years, had "equal validity" with English.

Welsh medium education also blossomed, with bilingual teaching in all primary schools and for at least a year in secondary schools. In traditionally Welsh-speaking areas students got five years of Welsh, and since 2000 all Welsh schools much teach the language to students up to the age of 16. Today, increasing numbers of schools across the land teach all subjects in the Welsh language; early objections from some non-Welsh-speaking parents that their children were being "forced" to learn a "dead" language have largely abated. Welsh-language university courses are also becoming more popular, so, for pretty much the first time in Wales' history, it is possible to be educated in Welsh from nursery to degree level. The other modern cornerstone for developing Welsh has been broadcast media. The BBC Welsh-language Radio Cymru began in the late 1970s, to be joined – after a considerable battle – by the S4C TV station in 1982. Together, they have sponsored and programmed popular Welsh learners' programmes and given the old language greater space than it has ever enjoyed before. Welsh-language classes are now offered right across the country, as well as in language centres across Britain and universities in Europe and North America.

## Speaking Welsh

Although Welsh words (and place names in particular) can appear bewilderingly incomprehensible, the rules of the language are far more strictly adhered to than in English. Thus, mastering the basic constructions and breaking words down into their constituent parts means that pronunciation need not be anywhere near as difficult as it may first appear.

The Welsh alphabet is similar to the English, though there are no letters j, k, v, x and z – except in occasional words appropriated from other languages. As well as the five English vowels, Welsh has y and w. Most vowels have two sounds, long and short: *a* is long as in *car*, short as in *fat*; *e* long as in *there*, short as in *pet*; *i* long as in *sea*, short as in *tin*; *o* long as in *more*, short as in *dog*; *u* roughly the same as a Welsh *i*; *w* long as in *soon*, short as in *look*; *y* long as in *sea* and short as in *bun* or *pin*. A circumflex over any vowel lengthens its sound. Adjoining vowels are generally pronounced as the two separate sounds, with the stress generally on the first.

Welsh consonants are pronounced in similar ways to English, except *c* and *g* are always hard as in *cat* and *gut* (never soft as in *nice* or *rage*), and *f* is always pronounced as *v* as in *vine*. Additional consonants are *ch*, pronounced as in German or as in *loch*; *dd*, pronounced as a hard *th* as in *those*; *ff* and *ph* as a soft *f* as in *five*; and *si* as in *shoe*. The Welsh consonant that causes most problems is *ll*, featured in many place names such as Llawhaden. This has no direct parallel in English, although the *tl* sound in *Bentley* comes close. The proper way to pronounce it is to place the tongue firmly behind the top row of teeth and breathe through it without consciously making a voiced sound.

## Useful Welsh words and phrases

**Hello** shwmae
**Good morning** bore da
**Good afternoon** p'nhawn da
**Good evening** noswaith dda
**Good night** nos da
**How are you? (formal)** sut ydych chi?
**How are you? (informal)** sut ywt ti?
**Please** os gwelwch chi'n dda
**Thank you** diolch
**You're welcome** croeso
**Excuse me** esgusodwch fi

**Open** ar Agor
**Closed** ar Gau
**Bus** bws
**Castle** castell
**Church** eglwys
**Cwm** valley
**Farm** fferm
**Hospital** ysbyty
**Hotel** gwesty
**Mile** milltir / filltir
**Museum** amgueddfa
**Police** heddlu
**Road** ffordd
**School** ysgol
**Shop** siop
**Slow** araf

The use of **Yes** and **No** in Welsh is a little more complicated, with differing forms of each depending on context. While not correct in all circumstances, **ie** for yes and **na** for no are used colloquially, and you will be understood if you follow suit.

## Welsh numbers

**1** un
**2** dau (fem. dwy)
**3** tri (fem. tair)
**4** pedwar (fem. pedair)
**5** pump
**6** chwech
**7** saith
**8** wyth
**9** naw
**10** deg
**11** un-deg-un
**12** un-deg-dau
**13** un-deg-tri
**20** dau-ddeg
**21** dau-ddeg-un
**22** dau-ddeg-dau
**30** tri-deg
**40** pedwar-deg
**50** pum-deg
**60** chwe-deg
**70** saith-deg
**80** wyth-deg
**90** naw-deg
**100** cant
**200** dau gant
**1000** mil

SMALL PRINT

## Publishing Information
First edition 2022

**Distribution**
*UK, Ireland and Europe*
Apa Publications (UK) Ltd; sales@roughguides.com
*United States and Canada*
Ingram Publisher Services; ips@ingramcontent.com
*Australia and New Zealand*
Booktopia; retailer@booktopia.com.au
*Worldwide*
Apa Publications (UK) Ltd; sales@roughguides.com

**Special Sales, Content Licensing and CoPublishing**
Rough Guides can be purchased in bulk quantities at discounted prices. We can
create special editions, personalised jackets and corporate imprints tailored to
your needs. sales@roughguides.com.
roughguides.com

Printed in Spain

A catalogue record for this book is available from the British Library
The publishers and authors have done their best to ensure the accuracy and
currency of all the information in **Pocket Rough Guide Pembrokeshire**, however,
they can accept no responsibility for any loss, injury, or inconvenience sustained
by any traveller as a result of information or advice contained in the guide.

## Rough Guide Credits

**Editor:** Annie Warren
**Author:** Owen Morton
**Cartography:** Carte
**Picture editor:** Tom Smyth
**Layout:** Katie Bennett

**Original design:** Richard Czapnik
**Head of DTP and Pre-Press:**
Katie Bennett
**Head of Publishing:** Kate Drynan

## Acknowledgements
Owen would like to thank the fantastic team at Rough Guides, particularly Annie
Warren and Sarah Clark. Thanks also to Martin Brasher and Katherine Morton
for their invaluable proofreading, and most of all to Andrew Morton, Annie Clark,
Chris Clark and Lizzie Thomson for all those childhood holidays!

SMALL PRINT

# Biography

Owen Morton has been visiting Pembrokeshire regularly for at least 35 years, starting with annual family holidays in his childhood, so it was a delight for him to write this book and share his love for this beautiful corner of Wales. Based in North Yorkshire, he's a keen traveller and has worked on several other projects for Rough Guides. When not exploring the world, he entertains himself by writing a blog about 1980s cartoons. His favourite animal is the wonderfully expressive and permanently furious manul, native to Central Asia and sadly not Pembrokeshire. Follow him on Instagram at @owenmortonmanul.

# Help us update

We've gone to a lot of effort to ensure that this edition of the **Pocket Rough Guide Pembrokeshire** is accurate and up-to-date. However, things change – places get "discovered", opening hours are notoriously fickle, restaurants and rooms raise prices or lower standards. If you feel we've got it wrong or left something out, we'd like to know, and if you can remember the address, the price, the hours, the phone number, so much the better.

Please send your comments with the subject line "**Pocket Rough Guide Pembrokeshire Update**" to mail@uk.roughguides.com. We'll credit all contributions and send a copy of the next edition (or any other Rough Guide if you prefer) for the very best emails.

# Photo Credits

(Key: T-top; C-centre; B-bottom; L-left; R-right)

**Caffi y Ragna** 66
**Dinosaur Park** 16T
**Jill Tate/The Landmark Trust** 90/91
**Oakwood** 14B, 20T
**Pembrokeshire Llamas Ltd** 73
**Pembrokeshire Photography** 59
**Public domain** 17T
**Shutterstock** 12/13B, 18T, 19T, 28, 29, 33, 36, 37, 38, 39, 40, 43, 45, 46, 48, 50, 55, 60, 63, 67, 75, 76, 100/101
**The Canteen** 74
**The Daffodil Inn** 89
**Visit Pembrokeshire** 14T, 15T, 15B, 19B, 35, 47, 52, 54, 71
**Visit Wales/Crown Copyright** 1, 2T, 2BL, 2CR, 2BR, 4, 5, 6, 10, 11T, 11B, 12T, 12B, 12/13T, 16B, 18C, 18B, 19C, 20C, 20B, 21T, 21C, 21B, 22/23, 25, 27, 30, 31, 32, 42, 68, 83, 84, 86, 88
**Wild Lakes Wales** 61
**Wildlife Trust of South & West Wales** 17B

**Cover:** Stone stack on the beach at Newport **Alan Foster/Shutterstock**

# Index

NOTES